Cinnamon MORNINGS

& Raspberry TEAS

D0599299

Other books by Pamela Lanier (published by Lanier Publishing):

*The Complete Guide to Bed & Breakfasts, Inns
    and Guesthouses in the United States and Canada*
All-Suite Hotel Guide
Elegant Small Hotels
Elegant Hotels — Pacific Rim
Condo Vacations: The Complete Guide
Family Travel — The Complete Guide
Golf Resorts: The Complete Guide
Golf Resorts International
22 Days in Alaska

Cinnamon MORNINGS

& Raspberry TEAS

by

Pamela Lanier

LANIER PUBLISHING INTERNATIONAL, LTD.
PETALUMA, CALIFORNIA

Cover design by Toby Schmidt
Illustrations by Lisa Umlauf-Roese
Interior design by Jacqueline Spadero
Typeset by Futura Graphics

Printed in Canada on recycled paper

The information in this book was supplied in large part by the inns themselves and is subject to change without notice. We strongly recommend that you call ahead to verify the information presented here before making final plans or reservations. The author and publisher make no representation that this book is accurate or complete. Errors and omissions, whether typographical, clerical, or otherwise, may sometimes occur herein.

This book may not be reproduced in whole or in part in any form or by any means, electronic or mechanical, including photocopying, recording, or by any information storage and retrieval system now known or hereafter invented, without written permission from the publisher.

© 1997 by Lanier Publishing International, Ltd. All rights reserved.
Published 1997.
ISBN 0-89815-960-1

This book can be ordered by mail from the publisher. Please include $2.75 for postage and handling for each copy. *But try your bookstore first!*
Lanier Publishing International, Ltd.
P.O. Box D
Petaluma, CA 94953
Tel. (707) 763-0271
Fax (707) 763-5762

In a nationwide survey of innkeepers conducted by *Innsider Magazine*

Rated #1
GUIDEBOOK
by Innkeepers
nationwide

This book is dedicated to our children and the hope that the earth they inherit will be as beautiful and bountiful as the one we enjoy.

Many thanks to the cooks who took time to send us their recipes and suggestions and to those inns who provided us with line drawings of their establishments.

Special thanks to all my friends who helped with this book, and especially Judy Jacobs, project coordinator, Karen Young Joffe, culinary editor, and Mariposa Valdes, lead editor, whose excellent work is evident throughout.

Contents

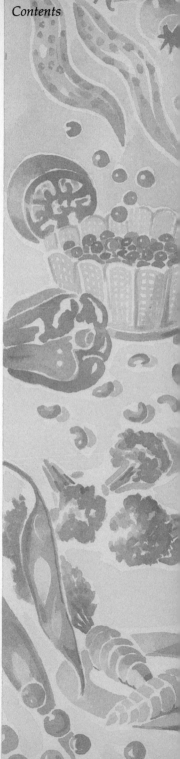

Bed and breakfast inns (B&Bs) allow the traveller to be immersed in the elegance of an antebellum plantation, to sleep in an historic landmark, to get away from it all on a Colorado ranch or to try houseboating in San Francisco. Whatever the setting, the personal and convivial atmosphere of a B & B provides the chance to make new friends and relax while vacationing. All the little B & B extras that one doesn't expect from an impersonal hotel add up to a special travel experience that is winning over all who travel the B & B route.

Of course, breakfast is an essential ingredient in the B & B experience. This cookbook is a collection of innkeepers' favorite recipes of outstanding regional American cuisine, from Southern biscuits and pecan pie to Northeastern blueberry muffins to Southwestern huevos rancheros. And because brunch, teatime and the cocktail hour are also common culinary customs in America's inns, we include B & B dishes to be served at these times as well. Some will spark the imagination of even the most discriminating gourmet, while others will be perfect for that hectic Sunday morning when you want to do something special but haven't got much time or energy.

Most of the recipes are simple and easy to prepare, but they cover a wide range of cooking styles from a diverse variety of kitchens. Some chefs are precise and detailed in their instructions; others leave much up to the individual cook. To make the preparation of the dishes easier, we have endeavored to standardize the measurements and procedures— without detracting from the unique style of each contributing chef. In addition to the recipes, we have included a short profile of each inn, along with reservation information, to help you with your future travel plans. When you visit each inn, you can taste its specialties for yourself.

Where two recipes from the same inn follow one another, reservation information follows the second recipe. Our charge-card key is as follows: MC equals MasterCard, AE equals American Express, V equals Visa, DC is Diner's Club, CB is Carte Blanche.

A price code is shown to give you an idea of the inns' prices, which are subject to change. Generally, Inexpensive is under $40; Moderate is $40 to $80; Expensive is $80 to $125; Very Expensive is over $125.

Bon appetit and sweet dreams!

Introduction

BREAKFAST

Part 1

Breakfast

At the heart of every traveller's dreams is an inn where everything possible is done to please the guests. Thanks to abundant fresh produce and the creativity of their kitchens, America's innkeepers have created some of the most imaginative and delicious dishes ever to grace a breakfast table.

These recipes offer a glimpse of the diversity of America's regional cuisine. The style, of course, varies regionally as well as from inn to inn, but with the recipes on the following pages, you can create these treats over and over again.

The variety is not just in the food, however. There are just as many kinds of breakfasts as there are inns. Luxury establishments pride themselves on exquisite cuisine graciously presented. At the Red Clover Inn in Mendon, Vermont, the innkeeper—who is also the chef—delights his guests with candlelit breakfasts with classical music playing in the background. Country and small town inns often offer very substantial breakfasts with several choices of entrées, freshly baked fruit breads, juices and cereal. The call to breakfast at Captain Jefferd's Inn in Kennebunkport, Maine, is the theme music from *Upstairs/Downstairs*. Guests assemble around the edge of a banquet table flanked by a dozen hand-painted chairs, are personally introduced, and then are served by a white-jacketed waiter.

Other inns provide breakfast at small tables for individual parties, where the food is either served to your exact specifications or is the day's special dish. At Santa Fe's Grant Corner Inn, individual hearty breakfasts consist of separate sideboards: one for beverages, including several kinds of coffees and teas; another for cereals, granola and cornflakes; and the entrée. In addition, a plate of fresh fruit and a basket of sweet rolls and breads are served at your table.

Of course, food is not the only factor that contributes to an enjoyable eating experience. The mood of the meal is also created by the place setting, the china, the tablecloth, the vase of flowers in the center of the table and the smile on the host or hostess's face.

INNKEEPING DREAMS

Pamela Lanier's Hungarian Coffee Cake

1 cup white sugar
1 cup brown sugar
1 cup shortening (butter or
   margarine)
3 cups all-purpose flour
½ cup chopped nuts
1½ teaspoons cinnamon

1 cup buttermilk
2 eggs
1 teaspoon vanilla
½ teaspoon salt
1 teaspoon baking powder
1 teaspoon baking soda

Preheat oven to 350°. Combine the first 6 ingredients. Take out 1 level cup and set aside for topping.

To the remaining mixture add the second column of ingredients.

Mix will be slightly lumpy. Pour into 2"×8" cake or pie pans (2 or 3). Cover with the 1 cup of reserved nut mix and bake at 350° for 20 or 25 minutes. Do not over bake. Will stay fresh for 4 days. Serves 16.

I'm too busy visiting inns to run one, but like a lot of people, I've dreamed of becoming an innkeeper. If you share the dream, we have an information packet for prospective innkeepers you will like (and it's free!). Send a self addressed stamped envelope to:

> *Innkeeper Information*
> *c/o The Complete Guide to Bed and Breakfasts,*
>   *Inns and Guesthouses*
> *P.O. Box D*
> *Petaluma, California 94953*

or visit our website **www.travelguides.com** for new recipes and Innkeeper Dream information.

GLACIER BEAR B&B
4814 Malibu Road
Anchorage, Alaska
99517
(907) 243-8818

MC/V
Moderate

This lovely inn provides first class accommodations at reasonable rates. Central location only 1.2 miles from the airport and 3 miles to downtown. Hiking and biking trails abound with the convenience of bicycles on location. Eight person spa for guests to enjoy and relax. Airport pick-up available.

G L A C I E R   B E A R   B & B

Caramelized Apple French Toast

1 cup brown sugar
3 tablespoons light Karo
   syrup
6 tablespoons butter
3 Granny Smith apples,
   peeled, cored and sliced

18 slices day old white bread
6 eggs
2 cups milk
½ teaspoon vanilla

Preheat oven to 325 degrees.

Combine sugar, syrup and butter; boil in pan for one minute. Pour into greased 9 by 13-inch pan. Place sliced raw apples on top of caramel. Place bread 3 layers deep in pan. Mix eggs, milk and vanilla together. Pour over bread.

Refrigerate overnight. Bake for 45 minutes until brown and slightly puffy.

Serves 8–12.

R I C H M O N D   I N N
Sausage and Egg Casserole

1 pound sausage	1 teaspoon salt
½ pound grated sharp cheese	1 cup sour cream
½ teaspoon dry mustard	10 to 16 eggs (depending on
½ teaspoon paprika	crowd)

Preheat oven to 325°. Cook and drain sausage. Spray 2 or 3 quart dish with vegetable spray. Put half of the cheese on bottom of dish. Mix spices with sour cream and mix with sausage. Spread over grated cheese. (This much can be done the night before.) Beat eggs and pour over sausage mixture. Sprinkle remaining cheese on top. Bake at 325° for 25–30 minutes or until eggs are set. Serves 8 to 14.

W E S T   M O U N T A I N   I N N
Ooey Gooey

4 large slices of bread	2 cups grated Vermont cheddar cheese
4 tablespoons mayonnaise	
8 eggs, fried	1 teaspoon paprika

Spread slices of bread with mayonnaise. Top each slice with 2 fried eggs and grated Vermont cheddar cheese. Melt under a broiler. Lightly sprinkle paprika on melted cheese to enhance flavor and add color. Serves 4.

RICHMOND INN
101 Pine Avenue
Spruce Pine, North Carolina
28777
(704) 765-6993

Moderate

Luxurious accommodations in the heart of the most spectacular mountain scenery. The Inn is close to the Blue Ridge Parkway, which is the ideal place to stroll after a meal. A splendid time awaits you!

WEST MOUNTAIN INN
Off Route 313
Arlington, Vermont
05250
(802) 375-6516

MC/V/AE
Moderate

There's plenty to do around the West Mountain Inn: bicycling on beautiful country roads; swimming, fishing, canoeing and tubing on the Battenkill River; and hiking or wilderness cross-country skiing on woodland trails.

MILLBROOK, A COUNTRY INN

Pancakes à la Millbrook

2 cups all-purpose flour
1 teaspoon salt
2 tablespoons sugar
4 teaspoons baking powder
2 eggs, lightly beaten

2½ cups milk
2 tablespoons butter, melted
1 pint strawberries or rasp-
    berries (optional)

Mix flour, salt, sugar and baking powder in a large bowl. In another bowl, whisk eggs and milk together with a wire whisk. Stir in butter. Pour wet ingredients (eggs, milk and butter mixture) over dry ingredients (flour, salt, sugar and baking powder) and mix with a wooden spoon until just blended. The batter should be lumpy. Pour ¼ cup batter per pancake onto a hot griddle. (For blueberry or strawberry pancakes, sprinkle fresh blueberries or sliced fresh strawberries on the pancakes as soon as you pour the batter onto griddle.) Cook until cakes are full of air bubbles on top and lightly browned on underside. Flip over to brown the other side. Serves 6.

MILLBROOK INN
RFD Box 62, Route 17
Waitsfield, Vermont
05673
(802) 496-2405

MC / V
Expensive

Guests can relax in this charming six-room country inn's unhurried atmosphere and revel in its candlelit dinners.

Millbrook, A Country Inn
Waitsfield, Vermont

TEN INVERNESS WAY

Banana Buttermilk Buckwheat Pancakes

1 cup all-purpose flour
½ cup whole wheat flour
½ cup buckwheat flour
2 tablespoons sugar
1 teaspoon salt
1 teaspoon baking soda

4 teaspoons baking powder
2 eggs, lightly beaten
4 tablespoons butter, melted
1½ cups buttermilk
½ cup milk
2 ripe bananas, mashed

In a large bowl, combine all-purpose flour, whole wheat flour, buckwheat flour, sugar, salt, baking soda and baking powder. In another bowl, combine remaining ingredients. Add liquid mixture to the dry ingredients, stirring well. Drop by ⅓ cupfuls onto a 350° griddle. Serves 4 to 6.

STONEHURST MANOR

Cornmeal and Bacon Pancakes

⅓ cup yellow cornmeal
1 cup all-purpose flour
1 teaspoon salt
2 teaspoons baking powder
1 egg

1¼ cup milk
1 tablespoon bacon fat, melted
2 strips bacon, cooked and crumbled

Mix together cornmeal, flour, salt and baking powder. In a separate bowl, beat the egg, add milk and then bacon fat. Stir this mixture slowly into the dry ingredients, mixing well. The batter should be fairly thin; add more milk if necessary. Finally mix in crumbled bacon. Cook pancakes in a skillet or on a griddle. Serve with butter and maple syrup. Serves 4.

TEN INVERNESS WAY
10 Inverness Way
Inverness, California
94937
(415) 669-1648

No credit cards
Moderate

This five-room inn is located an hour or so north of San Francisco and not far from the scenic beauty of Point Reyes National Seashore.

STONEHURST MANOR
P.O. Box 1937
Rt. 16
North Conway,
New Hampshire
03860
(603) 356-3113

MC/V/AE
Moderate to very expensive

The elegance of another era pervades this beautiful 24-room English-style country inn with rooms in every price range. The Stonehurst Manor is situated on 33 pine-forested acres.

HERSEY HOUSE
451 North Main Street
Ashland, Oregon
97520
(503) 482-4563

No credit cards
Expensive

This four-room Victorian farmhouse is located in the center of Ashland, site of the renowned annual Shakespeare Festival.

THE MONTE CRISTO
600 Presidio Avenue
San Francisco, California
94115
(415) 931-1875

MC / V / AE
Moderate to
very expensive

Located in San Francisco's exclusive Presidio Heights district, this inn is within walking distance of restored Victorian shops, restaurants and antique dealers.

HERSEY HOUSE
Gingerbread Pancakes

This recipe comes from Dee Maaske, an actress who has performed with the Ashland Shakespeare Festival.

2½ cups all-purpose flour
5 teaspoons baking powder
1½ teaspoons salt
1 teaspoon baking soda
1 teaspoon cinnamon
½ teaspoon ginger

¼ cup molasses
2 cups milk
2 eggs, lightly beaten
6 tablespoons butter, melted
1 cup raisins

Sift together flour, baking powder, salt, soda and spices. Combine molasses and milk and add eggs, stirring to blend. Stir in melted butter. Add molasses mixture to dry ingredients. Stir only until moistened. Mix in raisins. Cook on a hot griddle, using ¼ cup batter for each pancake. Serves 8.

THE MONTE CRISTO
Gooseberry Pancakes

1 cup whole wheat pastry
    flour
½ cup buckwheat flour
½ cup unbleached all-
    purpose flour
3 teaspoons baking powder
1 teaspoon salt

1 tablespoon brown sugar or
    honey
3 eggs, lightly beaten
2 cups milk
1 stick (4 ounces) butter,
    melted
1 cup gooseberries,
    cooked or canned

Sift flours with baking powder, salt and sugar (not honey). Beat together eggs, milk and melted butter. If using honey, add it to the milk and eggs mixture. Combine liquids with dry ingredients, stirring until just barely mixed. Fold in gooseberries. Cook on a hot griddle or in a greased frying pan. Serve with maple syrup and butter. Serves 6.

HARBOR HOUSE BY THE SEA

Souffléed Apple Pancakes

¼ cup (½ stick) unsalted
    butter
2 tart apples, peeled, cored
    and thickly sliced
¾ cups half-and-half
½ cup all-purpose flour
¼ teaspoon salt
3 egg yolks, lightly beaten

2 tablespoons unsalted but-
    ter, melted and cooled to
    room temperature
3 egg whites
pinch of cream of tartar
pinch of salt
1 tablespoon sugar
1 tablespoon butter

Preheat broiler.

In a stainless steel sauté pan or enameled skillet, melt the butter and sauté the apple slices, turning them carefully while cooking so they do not break. Cook until tender (about 6 minutes).

In a bowl, combine half-and-half, flour, ¼ teaspoon salt, egg yolks (one at a time) and the melted butter. In another bowl, beat the egg whites with cream of tartar and salt until they hold soft peaks. Add the sugar and continue beating until the whites hold stiff peaks. Stir ¼ of the whites into the batter to lighten it, then gently fold in the remaining whites. Melt 1 tablespoon butter in a flameproof 10" skillet (with an 8" bottom) over moderate heat. When it is hot, add half of the batter, spreading it evenly with a spatula. Cook the pancake for 3 minutes. Arrange half of the apple slices decoratively over the pancake, and put the pancake under the broiler, 4" from the source of heat, for 2 to 3 minutes or until puffed and golden brown. Slide the pancake onto a serving plate and keep warm. Make another pancake in the same manner with the remaining batter and apple slices. Serve the pancakes with maple syrup. Serves 4 as a breakfast dish or 8 (cut pancakes into wedges) as a dessert.

HARBOR HOUSE
BY THE SEA
5600 South Highway #1
P.O. Box 369
Elk, California
95432
(707) 877-3203

No credit cards
Moderate

In the tiny Mendocino town of Elk, the Harbor House by the Sea has five rooms, four cottages and its own private beach.

HUMPHREY HUGHES
HOUSE
29 Ocean Street
Cape May, New Jersey
08204
(609) 884-4428

MC/V/AE
Expensive

A restored Victorian home
in the historic seaside town
of Cape May, the Hum-
phrey Hughes House
serves a special Sunday
breakfast.

HILL FARM INN
R.R. 2, Box 2015
Arlington, Vermont
05250
(802) 375-2269

MC/V
Moderate

Hiking, fishing and full
country breakfasts are just a
few of the pleasures await-
ing guests at this seven-
room, three-cabin establishment, which has been in
operation for more than 75
years.

HUMPHREY HUGHES HOUSE

Golden Granola

1½ cups Quaker Old-Fashioned Oats	½ teaspoon cinnamon
½ cup chopped nuts, any kind	⅛ cup butter, melted
½ cup shredded coconut	⅛ cup honey
	½ teaspoon vanilla
	½ cup raisins or dried fruit

Preheat oven to 350°.

Mix oats, nuts, coconut and cinnamon in an ungreased baking dish. (To increase crispiness, one cup of cornflakes can be substituted for 1 cup of oats.) Combine melted butter, honey and vanilla. Pour over dry ingredients and mix. Bake granola for 30 to 40 minutes, stirring every 5 to 10 minutes to prevent burning. When evenly golden-colored, remove and, while cooling, add raisins or fruit. Serves 12. Recipe can be doubled and stored in tightly-covered containers.

HILL FARM INN

Hill Farm Inn French Toast

4 eggs	½ teaspoon vanilla
1 cup milk	8 slices homemade white bread, cut thickly
4 teaspoons sugar	
¼ teaspoon salt	

In a 13" by 9" baking dish, beat eggs, milk, sugar, salt and vanilla until fluffy. Add bread to dish, turning after it has soaked up about half of the mixture. When the bread is thoroughly soaked, use a pancake turner to transfer it to a hot buttered griddle (370°). Cook about 4 minutes on each side, or until golden brown. Serve with Vermont maple syrup. Serves 4 to 8.

THE SWAG

Swag Granola Cereal

1½ cups rolled oats
¼ cup sesame seeds
½ cup sunflower seeds
½ cup shredded unsweetened
    coconut
½ cup wheat germ
¼ cup bran

½ cup almonds
¼ cup oil
¼ cup honey
½ teaspoon vanilla extract
½ teaspoon almond extract
raisins or other dried fruit,
    as desired

Preheat oven to 300°.

Tumble together oats, sesame seeds, sunflower seeds, coconut, wheat germ, bran and almonds in a big bowl. Heat oil and honey together in saucepan until thin and fairly hot. Remove from heat and stir in vanilla and almond extracts. Pour over dry ingredients and stir to coat evenly. Spread in single layers on jelly roll pans and toast in oven, stirring from time to time, until evenly browned. Remove from oven and allow to cool thoroughly. Stir in raisins or other dried fruit. Serves 8 to 10. Recipe can be doubled and stored in tightly-covered containers.

THE SWAG
Route 2, P.O. Box 280-A
Waynesville,
North Carolina
28786
(704) 926-0430

MC/V
Moderate

A rustic hewn-log lodge located on a breath-taking mountaintop clearing. The Swag serves meals that are as impressive as the surroundings.

The Swag
Waynesville, North Carolina

GRANT CORNER INN
Dutch Babies

¼ cup butter
3 eggs
¾ cup milk
¾ cup all-purpose flour

banana topping (see
   following recipe)
2 cups lightly sweetened
   whipped cream

Preheat oven to 425°.

Put butter in a large cast-iron skillet and put skillet in hot oven. While butter is melting, beat eggs with electric mixer set at high speed for one minute. Whisk in milk alternately with flour, just until blended (may be slightly lumpy). Remove hot skillet from oven and pour batter onto melted butter. Bake 20 to 25 minutes or until brown and puffy. Dust with powdered sugar and serve immediately with banana topping and lightly sweetened whipped cream. Serves 4.

BANANA TOPPING
3 ripe bananas
3 tablespoons lemon juice
2 teaspoons cinnamon

pinch of nutmeg
banana brandy

Chop bananas, add lemon juice, cinnamon and nutmeg. Blend in banana brandy to taste.

Grant Corner Inn
Santa Fe, New Mexico

GRANT CORNER INN
122 Grant Avenue
Santa Fe, New Mexico
87501
(505) 983–6678

MC / V
Expensive

This elegant colonial home is set in one of America's most charming western towns.

F A I R H A V E N   I N N
Orange Tipsy French Toast

6 eggs, lightly beaten
2 tablespoons light cream
pinch of salt
2 tablespoons Triple Sec
    liqueur
1 tablespoon maple syrup

1 teaspoon grated orange
    rind
½ teaspoon grated nutmeg
1 baguette of French bread,
    thinly sliced

In a bowl, mix together all ingredients except bread slices. Soak bread in liquid mixture until all has been absorbed, turning the slices once. Cook on a hot griddle in cooking oil, turning to brown both sides. Serve with syrup and butter. Serves 6.

T H E   S M I T H   H O U S E
Smith House Banana Fritters

cooking oil
2⅓ cups all-purpose flour
½ teaspoon baking
    powder
½ teaspoon baking soda
½ teaspoon salt

2 eggs
½ cup sugar
two 13-ounce cans
    evaporated milk
12 bananas, peeled and
    quartered

Fill deep fryer with oil 4 to 5 inches deep and preheat oil to 375°.

Sift flour, baking powder, baking soda and salt together. In a separate bowl, beat together eggs and sugar. To egg mixture add milk alternately with sifted dry ingredients. Beat lightly after each addition to form a thin batter. Dip bananas into the batter and then drop them into hot oil. Fry, turning occasionally, until golden brown. Serves 10 to 12.

This batter can also be used for apple fritters: add ½ teaspoon cinnamon and ½ teaspoon nutmeg to batter and substitute peeled apple slices for banana quarters.

FAIRHAVEN INN
Rt. 2, Box 85
North Bath Road
Bath, Maine
04530
(207) 443–4391

No credit cards
Moderate

Using Fairhaven Inn as a base, guests can participate in a wide variety of outdoor activities, including hiking, ocean swimming, golfing, boating, fishing, skiing and snowshoeing.

THE SMITH HOUSE
202 Chestatee Street, S.W.
Dahlonega, Georgia
30533
(706) 867-7000

MC/V/AE
Inexpensive

Northern Georgia's Smith House offers Southern hospitality and all-you-can-eat home cooking.

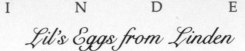

L I N D E N

Lil's Eggs from Linden

4 squirts Pam™ vegetable
   cooking spray
4 eggs

4 teaspoons half-and-half
2 tablespoons grated
   cheese

Preheat oven to 450°. Spray 4 muffin tins with Pam™.

Drop a raw egg into each tin. Cover each egg with a teaspoon of half-and-half. Sprinkle grated cheese over the top. Bake for 10 minutes. Gently remove eggs from tin and place on plates. Serves 4.

Lil's Grits from Linden

1 quart water
½ cup regular grits
1 cube beef bouillon

½ stick (4 tablespoons)
   butter
salt to taste

In a saucepan, bring the water to a boil. Stir in the grits, bouillon cube and butter. Cook for 15 to 20 minutes, stirring frequently. Consistency should be slightly thick, but not soupy. Add salt to taste. Serves 4.

LINDEN
1 Linden Place
Natchez, Mississippi
39120
(601) 445–5472

No credit cards
Expensive

An antebellum Southern mansion with a doorway used in the filming of *Gone With the Wind*, the Linden is noted for its outstanding collection of federal-period antique furniture and has been awarded Four Diamonds by Mobil.

Linden
Natchez, Mississippi

E D S O N   H I L L   M A N O R

L'Omelette Homard Forestier
(Omelette with Lobster and Mushrooms)

butter
4 ounces sliced mushrooms
salt and pepper, to taste
¼ cup good port
¼ cup heavy cream

1 fresh lobster tail, poached,
    shelled and diced (ap-
    proximately 1 cup)
1 ounce clarified butter
2 eggs, lightly beaten
freshly grated Parmesan
    cheese

Sauté mushrooms in butter. Season with salt and pepper. Stir in port and cream. Reduce by half. Add lobster meat and simmer just until the meat is warmed. To a seasoned omelette pan, add clarified butter. Heat the pan, and add the eggs. Stir briskly with a fork to lighten the omelette as it cooks. Add the warmed lobster mixture to the center of the omelette. Fold the omelette over the mixture, slide onto a serving plate and sprinkle with Parmesan cheese. Serve immediately. Serves 2.

D A I R Y   H O L L O W   H O U S E

Apple-Brie Cheese Omelette

½ apple, peeled, cored and
    thinly sliced
2½ tablespoons butter
2 eggs, room temperature

2 teaspoons cream or milk
dash of salt and pepper
2 tablespoons diced Brie
    cheese

Sauté apples in one tablespoon butter in a 5″ or 6″ omelette pan. Beat together eggs, cream or milk, and salt and pepper until blended but not frothy. Melt remaining butter in omelette pan over high heat until foam begins to recede (but before beginning to color). Pour in egg mixture and prepare omelette, beating to lighten but still allowing it to set on bottom. Fill with sautéed apples and cheese cubes. Fold or roll and slide out of pan onto a heated plate. Serves one.

EDSON HILL MANOR
1500 Edson Hill Road
Stowe, Vermont
05672
(802) 253-7371

MC / V
Expensive

Cross-country skiing, horse-back riding, swimming, hiking and barbecues await visitors to this secluded 400-acre country estate.

DAIRY HOLLOW HOUSE
515 Spring Street
Eureka Springs,
Arkansas
72632
(501) 253-7444

MC / V / AE
Expensive

The Dairy Hollow House is a transformed Ozarks farmhouse filled with folk art and flowers in every room. Its restaurant serves "Noveau (*sic*) Zarks," country cuisine with a French accent.

BLUE HARBOR HOUSE
Fat Free Stuffed French Toast

BLUE HARBOR HOUSE
67 Elm Street
Camden, Maine
04843
(800) 248-3196
(207) 236-3196

MC/V
Moderate

This restored 1835 home-
stead is filled with comfortable, antique furnishings.
Authentic country charm
and warm, friendly hospi-
tality awaits.

Stuffing:
6 ounces fat free cream cheese
6 ounces fat free yogurt
3 ounces fat free sour cream
12 slices whole wheat bread,
    crusts removed
powdered sugar
Maine maple syrup

Fruit:
1 cup fresh Maine blueberries
½ cup frozen raspberries,
    crushed

Batter:
2 packages 8 ounce Egg
    Beaters
1 cup skim milk
1 teaspoon vanilla

In a separate bowl mix stuffing ingredients. In a separate bowl mix batter ingredients. Coat six slices of bread with stuffing and place stuffing side up in large pan. Sprinkle fruit generously on top of stuffing. Coat remaining six slices with stuffing and place stuffing side down on top of fruit, making a sandwich.

Pour batter over sandwiches and soak for thirty minutes. Cook on grill at medium heat until golden brown, turning several times. Slice diagonally, place on large plate and serve hot with powdered sugar and Maine maple syrup.

Serves 4.

Blue Harbor House
Camden, Maine

SHADY LANE B & B

Italian Eggs in Tomatoes

4 large ripe tomatoes
1 tablespoon chopped garlic
4 tablespoons chopped fresh
    basil
2 tablespoons olive oil
salt and freshly ground pepper
4 large eggs
4 tablespoons grated
    parmesan cheese
parsley for garnish

Preheat oven to 425 degrees.

Cut off a small slice from the top of the tomatoes, and core tomatoes. Scoop out the pulp and reserve. Sprinkle the inside with salt and pepper. Turn upside down to drain. Chop the reserved pulp and add garlic, basil, olive oil, salt and pepper. Scatter the mixture evenly over the bottom of baking dish large enough to hold tomatoes snugly. Place the tomatoes right side up and break an egg inside each one. Sprinkle with salt, pepper and parmesan cheese.

Bake twenty minutes (do not let yolks become too firm). Garnish with parsley.

Serves 4.

SHADY LANE B&B
P.O. Box 314
Eagles Mere, Pennsylvania 17731
(800) 524-1248
(717) 525-3394

Moderate

A picturesque mountaintop resort near hiking, swimming, fishing, skiing and tobogganing. Eagles Mere is "the town time forgot." Summer craft and antique shops abound.

BAY AVENUE'S SUNSET
B&B
108 Bay Avenue
Cape Charles, Virginia
23310
(757) 331-2424

Most Credit Cards
Moderate

A waterfront escape on
Chesapeake Bay. Beautiful
sunsets, breezy porch, afternoon tea, and walking tours
all for guests to enjoy. Your
home away from home to
relax and unwind.

LA POSADA DE CHIMAYO
Sofia Trujillo's Red Chili

½ pound diced pork
2 cups water
3 garlic cloves
2 tablespoons fat
2 tablespoons all-purpose
    flour

1 heaping tablespoon ground
    red chili
salt to taste

Bring diced pork, water and garlic to a boil. Lower heat and
simmer for about ½ hour, until a nice broth forms. Strain,
reserving separately both meat and broth. Melt fat over
medium heat. Add flour and cook, stirring, for one minute.
Add ground red chili to flour mixture and cook one more
minute, sitrring constantly. Do not let burn! To the flour-
chili mixture, add pork broth gradually, stirring constantly;
then add the meat. Simmer for 10 to 15 minutes on low
heat, stirring occasionally. Salt to taste. Red Chili should be
the consistency of a thin gravy. Serve over fried eggs with
sausage and fried potatoes. Enough for 4 toppings.

BAY AVENUE'S SUNSET B & B
Overnight Grits and Sausage Casserole

1½ pounds mild bulk sausage
¾ cup uncooked quick-cooking
    grits (not instant)
6 eggs, beaten
1 cup plus 2 tablespoons milk
¼ teaspoon garlic salt
¼ teaspoon pepper

2 tablespoons margarine,
    softened
1 slice white bread, crusted
    and cubed
1½ cups (6 ounces) shredded
    extra sharp cheddar cheese

Cook the sausage over medium heat until browned, stirring
to crumble. Drain well and set aside. Cook grits according to
package. Set aside. In a large bowl, beat eggs, add milk, garlic
salt and pepper; beat again. Stir in softened margarine and
white bread pieces. Stir in shredded cheese and cooked grits
until cheese starts to melt. Stir in cooked, drained sausage.

BAY AVENUE'S SUNSET B & B

Refrigerate overnight, well covered.

In the morning spread mixture in lightly greased 9 by 13 inch baking dish. Bake in preheated oven at 350 degrees, uncovered one hour or until set. Let cooked casserole cool for 10–15 minutes before serving for ease in cutting and serving. Excellent served with fruit compote or fruit salad.

Serves 8–10.

THE REDSTONE INN

Huevos Redstone

½ onion, diced
1 stalk celery, diced
½ green pepper, diced
1½ tablespoons paprika
1½ tablespoons chili powder
½ teaspoon cumin
½ teaspoon black pepper
½ teaspoon salt
½ teaspoon garlic, minced
½ teaspoon oregano

½ teaspoon Cayenne pepper
½ tablespoon chicken base
1 tomato, diced
1 quart water
1 tablespoon cornstarch
8 eggs
8 corn tortillas
2 cups grated cheddar cheese
1 cup sour cream

THE REDSTONE INN
82 Redstone Boulevard
Redstone, Colorado
81623
(970) 963-2526

MC/V/AE
Moderate

The historic Redstone Inn was built in 1902 to house miners in a unique village created by a coal baron to prove his theory that people who live in pleasant surroundings are more productive. Today the 35-room inn offers such activities as horseback riding and skiing.

In a saucepan, sauté onion, celery and green pepper until onions are translucent. Stir in the seasonings, chicken base and diced tomato. Add 3 cups water, bring to a boil and simmer for 20 to 30 minutes. Mix cornstarch with remaining cup of water, add to pan and simmer for another 10 minutes. (This sauce is also great for topping chili rellenos or burritos or as a dip with corn chips.)

Fry eggs. Heat corn tortillas until tender. On an oven-proof serving plate, place 2 tablespoons sauce and cover with a tortilla. Top tortillas with egg and smother with sauce. Top with grated cheese and put under broiler until cheese is melted. Top with sour cream and serve.

Serves 8.

THE UNION HOTEL

Sausage

4 pounds freshly ground
  pork
¾ tablespoon salt
½ tablespoon freshly ground
  pepper

¾ tablespoon powdered sage
¾ tablespoon fresh ground
  Cayenne pepper
⅛ cup finely chopped garlic

Mix all ingredients together thoroughly with your hands and form into 3″ patties. Cook in a skillet until nicely browned. Serves 20.

Cream Biscuits

2 tablespoons baking
  powder
4 cups all-purpose flour
1 teaspoon salt

¼ pound good quality butter
  (salted, not sweet)
1 pint plus 1 tablespoon
  heavy cream

Preheat oven to 400° (or 425° if your oven is slow). Butter a baking sheet and set aside. Stir together the first 3 ingredients. Cut the butter in coarsely. Add the cream gradually. Knead briefly—just long enough to make a stiff dough. Do not over-work. Roll out to ½″ thickness. Cut into squares of desired size. (Cut-dough biscuits hold for 6 hours in the refrigerator. Do not freeze.) Bake 18 minutes, or until puffed and golden in color. Serve immediately. Makes 20 biscuits.

THE UNION HOTEL
401 First Street
Benicia, California
94510
(707) 746-0100

All major credit cards
Expensive

Located in an artists' colony not far from San Francisco. The Union Hotel's 12 individually-decorated rooms will delight lovers of Americana, and all will enjoy the hotel's traditional American cuisine.

OLD THYME INN

Plum Coffee Cake

1½ cups sugar
½ cup canola oil
2 eggs
1 cup whole milk
3 cups all-purpose flour
3 teaspoons baking powder
1 teaspoon salt
6–8 fresh plums, pitted &
    sliced

Topping:
1 cup brown sugar, packed
6 tablespoons all-purpose
    flour
1½ teaspoon cinnamon
6 tablespoons butter
1 cup chopped walnuts

Preheat oven to 350 degrees. In mixing bowl, cream sugar, oil and eggs until fluffy. Stir in the milk. Sift together the flour, salt and baking powder. Beat into other mixture. Spread batter in greased and floured 9 by 14-inch glass pan. Top with rows of plum slices. Combine remaining ingredients and mix until crumbly. Sprinkle crumbs over plums.

Bake approximately for 1 hour or until tested done. Cut into squares and serve warm. Serves 10–12.

OLD THYME INN
779 Main Street
Half Moon Bay, California
94019
(415) 726-1616

Most Credit Cards
Expensive

An 1890 Victorian inn with colorful herb garden on Main Street. Whirlpool tubs and fireplaces found in some rooms. Substantial fresh breakfasts.

Old Thyme Inn
Half Moon Bay, California

ELK COVE INN

Fluffy Two-Cheese Omelette

2 tablespoons butter
5 eggs
¼ cup half-and-half or milk
pepper to taste
2 tablespoons finely chopped
    chives or scallion tops

½ cup grated Tillamook
    cheddar cheese
½ cup grated Turumna
    cheese, or any semi-soft,
    rich white cheese

Preheat oven to 350°.

Heat butter in a heavy skillet. Beat eggs and half-and-half with an electric beater until extremely frothy. Immediately pour into skillet. Sprinkle with pepper and chives. Evenly distribute the 2 cheeses over the top. Cook, tightly covered, about 8 to 10 minutes, or until firm on top. With a spatula, cut the omelette into quarters. Turn 2 quarters over and onto remaining quarters to make 2 separate portions. Serves 2.

Orange Soufflé Omelette

2 tablespoons butter
5 eggs, separated
dash of cream of tartar
1 tablespoon sugar
2 tablespoons all-purpose flour
½ teaspoon baking powder
½ teaspoon dried orange peel
    or lemon peel

½ cup freshly squeezed and
    strained orange juice
1 cup sour cream
1 cup whole berry cranberry
    sauce
garnish of orange slices

Preheat oven to 350°.

Blend sour cream with cranberry sauce and set aside. Melt the butter in a heavy cast-iron skillet. Beat egg whites with cream of tartar and sugar until stiff. Blend the flour, baking powder and orange peel in a bowl. Stir in orange juice and egg yolks and beat until frothy. Gently fold in beaten egg whites. Spread this mixture into the melted butter in the heated skillet. Cook, tightly covered, for about 8 minutes or until just firm. Cut into quarters. Turn each quarter carefully over in place, and cook another 5 minutes. Serve with cranberry-sour cream topping, either between the quarters or on the side. Garnish with orange slices. Serves 2.

ELK COVE INN
P.O. Box 367
Elk, California
95432
(707) 877-3321

No credit cards
Moderate to expensive

Hugging the northern Mendocino coastline, the nine-room Elk Cove Inn is an old-fashioned country establishment serving German and French cuisine.

V E N T A N A   I N N

Eggs Mousseline

Eggs Mousseline is Ventana's sous-chef Peter Charles's favorite egg dish.

6 brioche rolls	1 cup heavy cream, whipped
6 tablespoons shaved, smoked salmon	½ cup chopped fresh dill, or to taste
6 poached eggs	
1 cup hollandaise sauce, room temperature	

Re-warm brioches. Remove the tops and some of the soft center. Stuff each roll with a tablespoon of shaved smoked salmon and a poached egg. Prepare the mousseline sauce by folding together equal amounts of hollandaise and whipped cream. Fold in dill. Consistency will continue to resemble that of hollandaise sauce. Ladle sauce over the poached eggs in brioches.

Chef Charles suggests serving a sautéed tomato and spinach mixture on the side: He sautés tomato slices quickly on a clean griddle top and serves three per person. He prepares the spinach by melting clarified butter in a sauté pan, throwing in a pinch of minced garlic, and adding one handful per person of washed whole spinach leaves. Spinach is cooked just long enough to wilt. Serves 6.

VENTANA INN
Highway 1
Big Sur, California
93920
(408) 624–4812

All major credit cards
Very expensive

The dramatic California coastline is the setting for this elegant inn and its Mobil four-star restaurant.

THE KENWOOD INN
38 Marine Street
St. Augustine, Florida
32084
(904) 824-2116

MC / V
Moderate

The 15-room, 19th-century
Kenwood Inn is located just
minutes from the beach in
the heart of the oldest city in
the United States.

THE KENWOOD INN
Pineapple Bread

3 cups sifted all-purpose
    flour
4½ teaspoons baking powder
1½ teaspoons salt
½ cup sugar

1 egg, lightly beaten
1½ cups milk
4 tablespoons melted butter
1 small can crushed pine-
    apple, well drained

Preheat oven to 350°. Butter a 9½" by 5½" loaf pan.

Sift together flour, baking powder, salt and sugar. Combine egg, milk and melted butter, then add drained pineapple. Pour into flour mixture and stir just enough to moisten dry ingredients—do not beat. Turn into loaf pan and bake 50 to 55 minutes, or until tests done. Makes one loaf or 8 servings (16 slices).

*The Kenwood Inn
St. Augustine, Florida*

HOTEL STRASBURG

Hotel Strasburg's Fried Tomatoes

3 medium tomatoes, firm
   and not quite ripe
2 cups all-purpose flour
2 teaspoons, more or less,
   garlic powder
1 teaspoon ground cumin
   seed

salt and pepper
1 egg
¾ cup milk
butter

Slice tomatoes into slices ¼" to ⅜" wide. Combine flour with seasonings in a shallow bowl. In a separate dish, beat egg, add milk and stir to blend. Dip tomato slices in seasoned flour. Shake off excess flour and dip in egg/milk wash. Dip tomatoes one more time in flour mixture. Allow slices to stand for 10 minutes or more. Sauté in butter for about 2 minutes on each side, or until golden brown. Serves 4 to 6. Serve with either poached or sunny-side-up eggs, country sausage and whole hominy for a breakfast that will carry you through the day.

HOTEL STRASBURG
201 Holliday Street
Strasburg, Virginia
22657
(540) 465-9191

MC / V / AE / CB / DC
Moderate

Built originally in the 1890s as a private hospital, the Hotel Strasburg has 18 antique-appointed rooms.

THE OLD MINER'S LODGE

Miner's Lodge Breakfast

4 large russet potatoes,
   boiled, peeled and cubed
9 pieces bacon, fried crisp
   and crumbled
4 tablespoons butter

½ bell pepper, chopped
minced garlic to taste
salt and pepper
8 eggs, lightly beaten
1 cup grated cheddar cheese

Preheat oven to 350°.

Melt butter in a skillet, add potato cubes and bell pepper and brown slightly. Add garlic to potatoes. Add salt and pepper to taste. Pour eggs over potatoes and cook until eggs form soft curds, stirring constantly. Mix in crumbled bacon. Sprinkle grated cheese over the top. Place skillet in oven or under broiler until cheese is melted. Serves 6.

THE OLD MINER'S
LODGE
P.O. Box 2639
Park City, Utah
84060
(801) 645-8068

MC / V
Moderate to expensive

In the heart of a favorite recreation and ski area not far from Salt Lake City, the Old Miner's Lodge preserves the spirit of the days when the Lodge was built to house those seeking their fortunes in silver.

THE ABBEY
34 Gurney Street
Cape May, New Jersey
08204
(609) 884-4506

MC/V
Expensive

The Abbey, in the historic
resort community of Cape
May, is located just one
block from the Atlantic
Ocean.

T H E   A B B E Y

Sly Devil Eggs

6 hard-boiled eggs
¼ cup melted butter
½ teaspoon Worcestershire
   sauce
¼ teaspoon dry mustard
1 (2½ ounce) can deviled
   ham
3 scallions, minced

Preheat oven to 350°. Butter a 9″ casserole dish.

Cut eggs in half and remove yolks. Mix yolks with butter, Worcestershire sauce, mustard, ham and scallions, blending until smooth. Stuff mixture into egg-white halves. Arrange eggs in the casserole.

SAUCE:
¼ cup (½ stick) butter
¼ cup flour
2 cups milk
salt and pepper to taste
English muffins

Melt the butter in a saucepan. Stir in the flour to form a paste and cook for a minute or two. Whisk in the milk and season with salt and pepper. Heat until thickened. Pour the sauce over the eggs and sprinkle with grated cheese. (This can be assembled ahead of time, refrigerated overnight, and heated before serving.)

Bake for 20 to 25 minutes. Serve over toasted English muffins. Serves 6.

THE CAPTAIN LORD MANSION

Rick's Soft-Boiled Eggs

Take eggs cold from the refrigerator and poke each with a pin to make a small hole in the large ends. Place eggs in boiling water and boil for 5 minutes. (It is best to use a timer for this!) Remove the eggs and run them under cold water to stop the cooking action. Place each egg in an egg cup and cut off the tops with an egg topper.

Bev's Cranberry Bread

5 cups all-purpose flour
2½ cups sugar
1 teaspoon baking soda
3 teaspoons baking
  powder
2 teaspoons salt

2 eggs
2 cups fresh orange juice
8 tablespoons (1 stick) butter,
  melted
1 cup water
2 cups cranberries

Preheat oven to 325°. Grease 3 loaf pans and dust with flour.

Sift together flour, sugar, baking soda, baking powder and salt. In a large measuring cup, combine eggs, orange juice, melted butter and water. Make a well in the center of the dry ingredients. Using a whisk or large spoon, stir wet ingredients into well of dry ingredients until all is combined. Fold in cranberries and pour batter into the prepared loaf tins. Bake for one hour, or until bread tests done. Makes 3 loaves.

THE CAPTAIN LORD MANSION
P.O. Box 800
Kennebunkport, Maine 04046
(207) 967-3141

No credit cards
Expensive

This 16-room mansion considers itself "an intimate Maine coast inn" and keeps in touch with former guests through an annual newsletter.

EL PARADERO

Huevos Rancheros por Gringos

1 large onion, chopped
1 clove garlic, minced
1 tablespoon oil
one 4-ounce can chopped
    green chilies or 3 large
    fresh chilies, skinned and
    chopped
one 32-ounce can stewed
    tomatoes
one 8-ounce can tomato
    sauce
one 6-ounce can tomato paste
1 teaspoon sugar

1 teaspoon vinegar
1 teaspoon chili powder
¾ teaspoon cumin
¾ teaspoon oregano
½ teaspoon salt
½ teaspoon basil
1 bay leaf
freshly ground pepper to
    taste
6 medium-size flour tortillas
6 eggs
1 to 1½ cups shredded jack
    cheese

Preheat oven to 350°.

In large skillet, sauté onion and garlic in oil until limp. Add chilies, stewed tomatoes, tomato sauce, tomato paste, sugar, vinegar, chili powder, cumin, oregano, salt, basil, bay leaf and pepper. Mix well and cover. Let simmer over low heat for at least 2 hours. If sauce gets too thick, add water. Refrigerate. At serving time, wrap tortillas in foil and warm while reheating sauce. Poach eggs. Place warm tortilla on oven-proof plate and place poached egg in center. Spoon sauce over egg to cover tortilla. Sprinkle cheese over all and place in oven until cheese is melted. Serves 6.

EL PARADERO
220 West Manhattan
Santa Fe, New Mexico
87501
(505) 988–1177

MC/V
Moderate to expensive

A remodeled 1800 to 1850s adobe within walking distance of the plaza, this 12-room inn offers a hearty full-course breakfast, and wine and cheese in the afternoon.

THE HANFORD HOUSE

Jimmy's Favorite Nut Bread

2 large eggs
2 cups brown sugar
3½ cups all-purpose flour
1 teaspoon baking soda

1 teaspoon baking powder
¼ teaspoon salt
1 cup chopped walnuts
1¼ cups buttermilk

Preheat oven to 350°. Butter two loaf pans.

Beat eggs, add sugar and mix well. In a separate bowl, sift together flour, baking soda, baking powder and salt. Stir walnuts into dry ingredients. Add dry ingredients alternately with the buttermilk to egg-sugar mixture. Batter will be stiff. Pour into pans, and level the tops. Bake approximately 50 minutes. Test for doneness. (A cake tester or toothpick should come out dry.) Cool 10 minutes in pans, then turn out onto racks. This heavy nutbread freezes well and is best sliced thin. Also delicious toasted and spread with butter or whipped cream cheese. Each loaf serves 8 to 10.

THE HANFORD HOUSE
P.O. Box 1450
61 Hanford Street
Sutter Creek, California
95685
(209) 267-0747

MC / V
Moderate to expensive

This newly-built, 9-room inn is set in an historic California gold rush town.

The Hanford House
Sutter Creek, California

THE GREY WHALE INN
Apricot-Prune Coffee Cake

This recipe was a blue-ribbon winner at the 1983 Mendocino County (California) Apple Show and Fair.

BATTER:
¾ cup dried apricots
¾ cup pitted dried prunes
3 cups unsifted all-purpose
    flour
½ tablespoon baking powder
¾ teaspoon baking soda
¼ teaspoon salt
¾ cup softened butter
1½ cups sugar
4 eggs

½ tablespoon vanilla
1 cup sour cream
STREUSEL:
½ cup firmly packed light
    brown sugar
2 tablespoons softened butter
2 tablespoons all-purpose
    flour
1 teaspoon cinnamon
2 tablespoons powdered
    sugar (optional)

Preheat oven to 350°. Butter a 10″ tube pan and dust with flour.

Coarsely chop apricots and prunes. Toss to combine. Sift together flour, baking powder, baking soda and salt. Set aside. Beat butter until fluffy (about 3 minutes). Gradually beat in sugar, then eggs, one at a time. Add vanilla. Blend in flour mixture alternately with sour cream, beginning and ending with flour mixture. Blend just until batter is smooth. Gently fold in the prunes and apricots.

Mix together first 4 streusel ingredients with a fork until crumbly. (Will make approximately one cup of streusel.)

Turn ⅓ of the batter into the prepared tube pan, spreading evenly. Sprinkle with ⅓ of the streusel mixture. Repeat, layering the remaining batter and streusel twice. Bake 55 to 60 minutes, or until cake tester comes out clean. Let cool in pan about 20 minutes. Remove from pan to platter. Sift powdered sugar over top if desired. This cake can be served warm. Yields one cake, which serves 10 to 12.

THE GREY WHALE INN

Vanilla Streusel Coffee Cake

3 cups all-purpose flour
1½ teaspoons baking powder
1½ teaspoons baking soda
¼ teaspoon salt
1½ cups softened butter
1½ cups sugar
3 eggs
1½ cups sour cream

1½ teaspoons vanilla
¾ cup firmly packed brown
　　sugar
¾ cup chopped nuts
1½ teaspoons cinnamon
2 tablespoons vanilla mixed
　　with 2 tablespoons water

Preheat oven to 325°. Butter 10″ tube pan.

Sift together flour, baking powder, baking soda and salt, and set aside. Combine butter and sugar in large bowl and beat until fluffy. Add eggs one at a time, beating well after each addition. Blend in sour cream and vanilla. Gradually add sifted dry ingredients and beat well. Combine brown sugar, nuts and cinnamon in a separate bowl. Turn ⅓ of the batter into the tube pan and sprinkle with ½ of the nut mixture. Repeat. Add remaining batter and spoon diluted vanilla over top. Bake 60 to 70 minutes. Cool completely before removing from pan. (Texture will be moist.) Makes one cake, which serves 10 to 12.

GREY WHALE INN
615 North Main Street
Fort Bragg, California
95437
(707) 964–0640

MC/V/AE
Moderate to expensive

This historic north coast Californian landmark features ocean-view suites, antiques and an extensive art collection.

The Grey Whale Inn
Fort Bragg, California

THE TURNING POINT
Route 23
3 Lake Buel Road
Great Barrington,
Massachusetts
01230
(413) 528-4777

No credit cards
Moderate

Located not far from
Tanglewood and ski slopes,
The Turning Point has a
no-smoking policy and
serves vegetarian whole-
grain breakfasts.

HAWTHORNE INN
462 Lexington Road
Concord, Massachusetts
01742
(508) 369-5610

No credit cards
Expensive

Located on land that once
belonged to Ralph Waldo
Emerson, the Alcotts and
Nathaniel Hawthorne, the
inn is filled with antique
furnishings, handmade
quilts and sculpture created
by the innkeeper.

THE TURNING POINT

Turning Point Breakfast Muffins

1 cup whole wheat flour
1½ cups raw bran
1 teaspoon baking powder
1 teaspoon baking soda
¾ cup raisins
1 egg, lightly beaten
1 tablespoon oil or melted
    butter

¾ cup milk
¾ cup apple juice
2 tablespoons maple syrup or
    honey
cinnamon to taste
12 walnut halves

Preheat oven to 375°. Butter 12 muffin tins.

Mix together whole wheat flour, bran, baking powder, baking soda and raisins. Add the remaining ingredients, stirring well to incorporate them evenly. Divide dough into the 12 muffin tins. Top with walnut halves. Bake for about 15 minutes or until muffins test done. Serve hot. Yields 12 muffins.

HAWTHORNE INN

Brown Breakfast Bread

¾ cup honey
¾ cup molasses
3½ cups all-purpose flour
2 teaspoons baking soda
2 teaspoons ginger
2 teaspoons cinnamon

2 teaspoons allspice
dash of salt
2 cups milk
1 cup raisins
2 tablespoons orange
    marmalade

Preheat oven to 350°. Butter a large baking dish.

Beat together honey and molasses. Stir in remaining ingredients until just blended. Bake for 1¼ hours, or until done.

A N C H U C A

Overnight Coffee Cake

¾ cup softened butter
1 cup sugar
2 eggs
1 cup sour cream
2 cups all-purpose flour
1 teaspoon baking powder
1 teaspoon baking soda

½ teaspoon salt
1 teaspoon ground nutmeg
¾ cup firmly packed brown
  sugar
½ cup chopped walnuts or
  pecans
1 teaspoon ground cinnamon

Butter a 13" by 9" by 2" baking pan and lightly dust with flour.

Cream butter and sugar until light and fluffy. Add eggs and sour cream, mixing well. Combine flour, baking powder, baking soda, salt and nutmeg. Add to batter and mix well. Pour into baking pan. In a separate bowl, combine brown sugar, nuts and cinnamon. Mix well and sprinkle evenly over batter. Cover and chill overnight.

In the morning, uncover and bake at 350° for 35 to 40 minutes, or until cake tests done. Serves 15.

S C H W E G M A N N   H O U S E

Coconut Breakfast Bread

2¾ cups all-purpose flour
1¼ cups toasted flaked
  coconut
¾ cup sugar
1 tablespoon baking powder

1 teaspoon salt
1½ cups milk
3 tablespoons melted butter
1 teaspoon coconut extract

Preheat oven to 350°. Butter and flour a 9" by 5" by 3" pan.

Combine flour, coconut, sugar, baking powder and salt in a large bowl and make a well in the center of the mixture. Combine the remaining ingredients. Add the liquids to the dry mixture and stir until well moistened. Spoon into loaf pan. Bake for one hour or until tests done. Cool for 10 minutes in pan, then remove and cool completely on wire rack. Yields one loaf, which serves 8 to 10.

ANCHUCA
1010 First East Street
Vicksburg, Mississippi
39180
(601) 631-6800

MC / V / AE
Very expensive

Guests at Anchuca can immerse themselves in Southern splendor, sipping mint juleps by the swimming pool, relaxing in antique-furnished bedrooms and enjoying breakfast in the inn's magnificent dining room.

THE SCHWEGMANN
HOUSE
438 West Front Street
Washington, Missouri
63069
(314) 239-5025

MC / V
Moderate

This pre-Civil War building, with its 9 gracious antique-appointed rooms, sits on the banks of the Missouri River, just an hour's drive west of St. Louis.

THORNROSE HOUSE
531 Thornrose Avenue
Staunton, Virginia
(540) 885-7026
(800) 861-4338

Moderate

A stately Georgian resi-
dence with air conditioning
and private baths in all
guestrooms. Located in a
historic Victorian town. An
adjacent 300 acre park offers
golf, tennis, and swimming.

THORNROSE HOUSE

Low-Fat Cranberry Bran Muffins

2½ cups unbleached flour
2 tablespoons baking powder
½ teaspoon salt
⅔ cup sugar
3 cups fresh or frozen
    cranberries
2 cups all-bran cereal
2 cups skim milk
2 eggs
6 tablespoons oil

Preheat oven to 400 degrees.

In a large bowl whisk together flour, baking powder, salt and ⅓ cup sugar. Set aside. Process cranberries and second ⅓ cup of sugar in food processor briefly.

In a second large bowl combine milk and bran cereal to soak for three minutes. Mix in eggs and oil; stir in dry ingredients and cranberries mixing until moistened. Makes eighteen large muffins. Bake for approximately 25 minutes.

Makes 18 large muffins.

B R U N C H

Part 2

Brunch

This felicitous combination of breakfast and lunch should be slowly savored on a lazy morning. Whether enjoyed in an inn or your own home, the ingredients are the same: good food, pleasant surroundings and good conversation.

The Union Hotel in Benicia (an artist's colony not far from San Francisco) is a mecca for lovers of American cuisine. Brunch guests delight in scrapple, homemade sausage, grits, red plaid hash and scrumptious cream biscuits.

Brunch can be served as individually ordered entrées or as a buffet—a splendid idea for entertaining at home. Gramma's B & B Inn in Berkeley, California, presents so many buffet dishes that it's difficult to decide where to begin. Will it be green salad, crudités, paté, pasta salad, shirred eggs, sausage, home-fried potatoes, or a bit of each? You can greet your guests with a big pitcher of Bloody Marys and then slowly unveil the morning's delights. Whether you serve Shrimp Scampi Bicard, Crustless Quiche, Dill Bread or Buttermilk Pie, it's sure to be a meal to be remembered.

COLUMBIA CITY HOTEL

Shrimp-Shirred Eggs

3 tablespoons clarified butter
8 eggs
1 large shallot, chopped
1 cup brut champagne
1½ pounds frozen or fresh
   shrimp, peeled and
   deveined

3 cups heavy cream
¼ pound (1 stick) unsalted
   butter
8 olive rounds
salt and pepper to taste

Preheat oven to 350°. Butter a shallow, oven-proof casserole dish large enough to hold 8 eggs in a single layer.

Crack eggs in the casserole, being careful not to break the yolks. Dot yolks with 1 tablespoon clarified butter and bake uncovered in oven until the yolks are set.

Heat remaining 2 tablespoons clarified butter in a large skillet. Sauté the chopped shallots lightly in the butter. Add champagne and reduce by half. Add the shrimp and cook gently for 2 to 3 minutes. Remove shrimp with a slotted spoon and keep warm. Increase heat under skillet and reduce juices to a thin glaze. Blend in cream and simmer until mixture thickens, about 20 to 30 minutes. Remove from heat and whisk in ¼ pound (1 stick) butter, a tablespoon at a time. Stir in the reserved shrimp, season to taste and pour over the shirred eggs. Garnish with olive slices. Serves 4.

COLUMBIA CITY HOTEL
P.O. Box 1870
Columbia, California
95310
(209) 532-1479

MC/V
Expensive

Located in an historic gold rush town which is now a state park, the City Hotel's dining room and saloon serve as a training ground for students enrolled in the hotel management and culinary program of a nearby college.

NEW SHERIDAN HOTEL
231 Colorado Avenue
Telluride, Colorado
81435
(970) 728-4351

MC/V/AE
Moderate

The New Sheridan Hotel of
Telluride, a National Historic Landmark, is situated in
one of Colorado's most
beautiful towns.

WHITE CLOUD INN
RD1, Box 215
Newfoundland,
Pennsylvania
18445
(717) 676-3162

MC/V/AE/DC
Inexpensive

This retreat of 50 wooded
acres offers a swimming
pool, tennis court, peace of
mind and meatless natural-
foods cooking.

JULIAN'S AT THE NEW SHERIDAN
Spinach Frittata

2 eggs
½ cup cooked, drained and
   chopped spinach

2 tablespoons water
¼ cup warm tomato sauce
3 strips Mozzarella cheese

Combine eggs, spinach and water. Pour into hot, greased omelette pan and cook over medium heat until egg mixture sets. Remove from heat. Ladle sauce over cooked eggs. Place strips of cheese over top and place under broiler until Mozzarella melts. Serves 2.

WHITE CLOUD INN
White Cloud Cashew Soup

3 cups water or soup stock
1 cup cashew pieces
1 scant teaspoon curry
   powder
1 teaspoon salt

1 heaping teaspoon poultry
   seasoning
4 teaspoons chives for
   garnish
paprika to taste for garnish

Heat first five ingredients to boiling. Put in blender and blend until smooth. Reheat briefly and serve sprinkled with chopped chives and paprika. Yields 4 cups or 4 servings.

CAPTAIN MEY'S INN

Quiche Mey

6 eggs
2 cups heavy cream
½ cup fresh bread crumbs
½ teaspoon salt

¼ teaspoon nutmeg
2 tablespoons frozen orange
    juice concentrate
1 cup chopped spinach

Preheat oven to 350°. Butter a quiche dish.

Beat eggs and cream together. Stir in bread crumbs, salt, nutmeg, orange juice and spinach. Pour into quiche dish. Bake 40 minutes in oven or 20 minutes in microwave. Makes one quiche, which serves 8.

CAPTAIN MEY'S INN
202 Ocean Street
Cape May, New Jersey
08204
(609) 884-7793 and
(609) 884-9637

MC/V
Expensive

Named after this resort town's Dutch explorer-founder, the inn keeps the heritage of Holland alive, with a Delft Blue collection, Dutch artifacts and imported cheeses.

Captain Mey's
Cape May, New Jersey

GLENBOROUGH INN
AND COTTAGE
1327 Bath Street
Santa Barbara, California
93101
(805) 966-0589

MC / V
Moderate to very expensive

In the seaside resort community of Santa Barbara, the Glenborough Inn and Cottage has 8 antique-appointed rooms and suites and serves a full breakfast in bed.

GUSTAVUS INN
P.O. Box 60
Gustavus, Alaska
99826
(907) 697-2254

Expensive

A charming Inn with ocean view rooms near Alaska's famous Glacier Bay. The perfect setting for a relaxed getaway.

THE GLENBOROUGH INN

Momma's Egg Casserole

8 slices bread	4 ounces chopped chilies
7 eggs	3 cups grated sharp
2½ cups milk	cheddar
1 teaspoon oregano	3 cups grated jack cheese
½ teaspoon minced garlic	1 avocado, sliced
1½ teaspoons salt	½ cup sour cream

The night before, place slices of bread in a 9" by 12" buttered casserole dish. (Can also be placed in individual casseroles.) Spread the chilies over the bread. Mix together the eggs, milk, oregano, garlic and salt. Pour the egg mixture over the chilies. Sprinkle the cheeses over the entire dish. Cover and refrigerate overnight.

The next morning, preheat oven to 325°. Bake for 50 minutes or until puffy and barely set. (Bake individual casseroles for 15 minutes.) Serve immediately with avocado slices and sour cream garnish. Serves 8 to 12.

GUSTAVUS INN

Halibut or Salmon Parmesan

Preheat oven to 400°. Cut up your cleaned and skinned filets into serving sized pieces, roll in flour, then beaten eggs, then a mixture of 3 parts sourdough bread crumbs (any crumbs will work) and 1 part grated parmesan cheese.

Place on lightly greased open sided cookie sheet and bake at 400° for 15 to 20 minutes. Check for doneness by flaking apart and take out when just done to keep it from drying out. Serve with lemon wedges and cocktail sauce.

FOREST, A COUNTRY INN

Sherried Crab Quiche

9" pie crust (see following recipe)
4 tablespoons softened butter
2 cups heavy cream
4 eggs
1 teaspoon salt
¼ pound shredded Swiss cheese

2 tablespoons minced onion
two 6-ounce packages frozen snow crab, thawed and drained
2 tablespoons dry sherry
⅛ teaspoon Cayenne pepper

Preheat oven to 425°. Prepare pie crust and line a 9" pie plate with the crust. Spread crust with one tablespoon softened butter and set aside.

In a medium bowl, whisk together cream, eggs and salt until well blended. Stir in cheese. Over medium heat, melt remaining 3 tablespoons butter, add the onions and cook until softened (about 5 minutes). Stir onions, crab, sherry and Cayenne pepper into the egg-cream mixture. Pour into buttered pie crust (see following recipe). Bake for 15 minutes. Lower oven to 325° and bake 35 minutes longer, or until knife inserted in center comes out clean. Serves 8.

BUTTER PIE CRUST:
4 tablespoons butter
1 cup unsifted flour

1 egg yolk
5 teaspoons ice water

Cut butter into flour until mixture forms coarse crumbs. Lightly stir in egg yolk with a fork. Add water, a little at a time, and stir until pastry clings together. Form it into a ball and refrigerate for at least one hour before rolling it out.

FOREST, A COUNTRY INN
Route 16A
Intervale, New Hampshire 03845
(603) 356-9772

MC/V/AE
Expensive

In the heart of New Hampshire's White Mountains is Forest, A Country Inn, the place for traditional hospitality and old-fashioned relaxation.

F O X   S T A N D   I N N
Eggs à la Jean

This recipe is great for using up leftovers.

2 tablespoons butter
¼ cup chopped onion
¼ cup cubed baked potatoes
¼ cup broccoli pieces
¼ cup diced green pepper
¼ cup ham chunks
1 clove garlic, minced
1 tablespoon sherry

¼ teaspoon tarragon
¼ teaspoon basil
salt and pepper to taste
¼ cup cream
¼ cup shredded cheddar
   cheese
8 eggs

Preheat oven to 350 degrees. Butter a small casserole or 4 boat dishes.

Melt butter in a sauté pan. Sauté onion, potatoes, broccoli, peppers, ham and garlic until heated through. Add sherry and seasonings to taste, then mix in cream and cheese. Stir until cheese melts. Line a casserole or 4 dishes with this mixture, and top with eggs (2 per individual boat dish). Bake until egg whites are firm. Serve this dish with fresh fruit. Serves 4.

Q U E E N   V I C T O R I A   B & B
Cranberry Chutney

3 or 4 small oranges, peeled
   and sectioned
4 cups cranberries, washed
2 cups sugar
1 apple, unpeeled and chopped

½ cup orange juice
¼ cup chopped walnuts
1 tablespoon vinegar
½ teaspoon cinnamon
½ teaspoon ground ginger

Combine all ingredients in a pan and simmer gently. Cook only until cranberries pop open. Cool and store in a covered container in refrigerator.

The chutney is excellent as an accompaniment to cold meats. It is also lovely used as a filling for peaches or pears (canned or fresh) which are then heated and served as a festive side dish at breakfast. Makes 5 cups.

FOX STAND INN
R.R. 1, Box 108F
Royalton, Vermont
05068
(802) 763-8437

No credit cards
Inexpensive

The Fox Stand Inn and restaurant is an historic stagecoach stop built in 1818 on the banks of the White River.

QUEEN VICTORIA B&B
102 Ocean Street
Cape May, New Jersey
08204
(609) 884-8702

MC/V
Expensive

A country inn located in the center of the nation's oldest seaside resort. Specializes in comfort and service, as well as scrumptious, large breakfasts. Evening chocolate turndowns.

GRAMMA'S   B & B   INN

Cauliflower Custard in Swiss Chard Leaves

1 bunch Swiss chard
1 head cauliflower
1 onion, chopped
1 clove garlic, chopped
1½ cups cream or
    half-and-half
7 eggs

½ cup grated Parmesan
    cheese
½ cup grated mozzarella
    cheese
salt, pepper and nutmeg to
    taste

Preheat oven to 350°. Butter a ring mold.

Blanch the chard by placing leaves in a large pot of boiling water for a minute or so. Run under cold water, then drain on paper towels. Line ring mold with the leaves of chard, flopping the extra over the outside (you will fold them in later). Chop and cook the cauliflower. While cauliflower is cooking, sauté the onion and garlic. Set aside. Purée cauliflower in a blender or food processor with some of the cream. Add eggs and blend well. Add onion and garlic. Add cheeses, the remaining cream and seasonings. Mix well. Pour custard into the lined mold, lapping the leaves over the top and set pan in a *bain marie* filled with ½" of water. Cover the top of the mold with buttered wax paper. Bake for 25 to 30 minutes or until custard tests done. Loosen edges right away, but allow dish to stand for at least 5 minutes before turning mold out. Can be served hot or cold. Serves 6 to 8.

GRAMMA'S BED &
BREAKFAST INN
2740 Telegraph Avenue
Berkeley, California
94705
(510) 549-2145

MC/V
Expensive

Just a short walk from the University of California campus, Gramma's offers a Sunday champagne brunch.

PINE MEADOW INN
1000 Crow Road
Merlin, Oregon
97532
(800) 554-0806
(541) 471-6277

Moderate

This secluded country retreat is located on nine acres of meadows and woods near the Rogue River. A wraparound porch, gardens, koi pond lend to the friendly and comfortable environment.

PINE MEADOW INN
Light Fresh Veggie Frittata

½ cup asparagus tips
1 medium zucchini, sliced and quartered
1 cup fresh mushrooms, chopped
6 eggs
egg substitute equal to 6 eggs

2 cups nonfat cottage cheese
2 cups low-fat mozzarella cheese, grated
½ cup green onions, chopped
1 teaspoon fresh dill, snipped
extra dill for garnish
non-stick cooking spray

Preheat oven to 350 degrees. Lightly sauté asparagus tips, zucchini, and mushrooms. Be careful not to overcook. Combine the eggs and egg substitute and beat until light and fluffy. Mix in cottage cheese and mozzarella cheese. Add green onions, sautéed vegetables, and dill, mixing until well blended.

Pour mixture into a 9 by 13-inch baking dish prepared with non-stick cooking spray. Sprinkle top with more dill. Bake for 1 hour or until a knife inserted into the center comes out clean. When using individual ramekins, reduce baking time to 30 minutes. Recommend serving with a fresh chutney and toast.

Serves 8–10.

Pine Meadow Inn
Merlin, Oregon

SAGEBRUSH INN

Chili Rellenos

Rellenos may be served as an entrée or as an accompaniment to other Mexican foods.

enough cooking oil to fill deep fryer
12 to 16 chilies (fresh or canned)
½ to ¾ pound mellow cheese, such as Colby, Monterrey jack, or other mild cheese
4 cups flour

2 eggs
1½ cups beer
2 cups lukewarm water
½ teaspoon ground cumin
½ teaspoon salt
½ teaspoon Maggi liquid seasoning
1½ cups flour

Preheat 5 to 6 inches of oil in deep fryer to 350° to 375°.

Split the chilies lengthwise down the top and clean and remove seeds. Cut cheese into strips 4" long by 1" wide. Stuff chilies with cheese strips. With an electric mixer, blend flour, eggs, beer, water, cumin, salt and Maggi.

Dip the stuffed rellenos in additional flour, then in the batter. Fry until golden brown. Makes 12 to 16.

SAGEBRUSH INN
P.O. Box 557
Taos, New Mexico
87571
(505) 758-2254

MC/V/AE/DC
Moderate

This newly renovated 100-room adobe inn is furnished with handcarved Southwest furniture and little kiva fireplaces.

CRYSTAL ROSE INN

Cheese Strata

12 slices bread, cubed
2¼ cups grated cheese
3 cups milk
12 eggs
6 tablespoons melted butter

¾ teaspoon dry mustard
chopped ham (optional)
chopped green chilies (optional)

Preheat oven to 350°. Butter a baking dish.

Layer dish with bread and cheese, ending with cheese. (Chopped ham or green chilies may be layered into the bread and cheese for variety.) Combine milk, eggs, melted butter and mustard in blender for about 10 seconds. Pour over bread/cheese mixture and refrigerate overnight. Bake until firm in the center, about 45 to 60 minutes.

CRYSTAL ROSE INN
789 Valley Road
Arroyo Grande, California
93420
(805) 481-1854

MC/V/AE
Expensive

A majestic 107-year-old mansion on the edge of the Pacific, the Crystal Rose Inn is noted for beautiful gardens and gourmet meals served in the dining room under its crystal chandelier.

CLAUSER'S BED & BREAKFAST

Firehouse Omelet

12 eggs
1 cup rice, cooked in 2 cups
    water
1 stick butter, melted
1 cup ham, cubed
1 pound cottage cheese, small
    curd
1 package leek soup mix

1 teaspoon onion salt
1 teaspoon garlic salt
¼ teaspoon black pepper
1 package spinach, thawed,
    drained and squeezed of
    excess water
½ cup grated parmesan cheese

Preheat oven to 325 degrees.

In a large bowl, beat nine of the eggs, then add the cooked rice, melted butter, ham cubes, cottage cheese, soup mix, spices, drained spinach and mix together. Sprinkle ¼ cup of the grated parmesan cheese on the bottom of a 13 by 9 inch baking dish. Spread the rice and cottage cheese mixture in the dish. Beat the three remaining eggs and pour evenly over the top of the mixture. Sprinkle the remaining ¼ cup of cheese over mixture.

The dish may be covered and refrigerated several hours or overnight. Remove from refrigerator thirty minutes prior to baking. Bake for 40–50 minutes. Remove from oven and let cool 15–20 minutes before cutting. The omelet will have a consistency similar to quiche, but without a crust. It will cut nicely into squares.

Serves 12.

Note: For a vegetarian dish, leave out the ham. For variety, instead of ham, use cooked sausage, chopped salami or cooked and crumbled bacon.

CLAUSER'S BED &
BREAKFAST
201 E. Kicklighter Road
Lake Helen, Florida
32744
(800) 220-0310
(904) 228-0310

MC/V
Moderate

An 1880's Victorian home located in a tranquil country setting. Magnificent trees, heirlooms, quilts, linens and lace compliment your stay. "Everybody's grandmother's house."

SILVER WOOD B & B

Sour Cream Enchiladas

2 cans cream of chicken soup	1 pound lean ground beef
two 4-ounce cans chopped green chilies	¾ cup chopped onion
1 soup can water	1 teaspoon garlic salt
2 cups sour cream or sour half and half	2 dozen corn tortillas
	3–4 cups grated cheddar cheese

Preheat oven to 350 degrees. Combine soup, green chilies, water and sour cream. Warm, but do not boil. Reserve two cups of sauce. Brown ground beef with onion. Season with garlic salt and pepper to taste. Warm tortillas in microwave (fifteen seconds for four tortillas). Dip tortillas in the warm sauce. Place one tortilla in the casserole flat. Add 1 tablespoon ground beef mixture, approximately 1 tablespoon cheese and roll to make enchiladas. Repeat the procedure with remaining tortillas, placing them side by side in the casserole. Pour reserved sauce over the rolled enchiladas and top with additional cheese.

Bake 25–30 minutes. Makes two 9-inch by 13-inch casseroles. Freezes well.

Serves 8.

SILVER WOOD B&B
463 County Road 512
Divide, Colorado
80814
(719) 687-6784

Most credit cards
Moderate

The perfect getaway to relax and enjoy with glorious views from private decks. Nature trails abound. Enjoy a country gourmet breakfast and outstanding hospitality.

Silver Wood B&B
Divide, Colorado

DUNBAR HOUSE 1880

Chili, Cheese, Sausage Trio

two 4-ounce cans whole chilies
1 pound link sausage
½ pound Monterey jack cheese
1 pound cheddar cheese

one 13-ounce can evaporated milk
2 to 3 tablespoons all-purpose flour
1 teaspoon baking powder
8 eggs, beaten lightly
one 8-ounce can tomato sauce

Preheat oven to 350°. Butter a 3-quart casserole dish.

Cut chilies into strips. Cook and quarter sausages. Layer chilies, sausages and cheese in the casserole dish. Mix milk, flour, baking powder and beaten eggs and pour over layers. Bake 30 to 40 minutes. Drizzle tomato sauce over and bake 10 minutes more. Let set 10 minutes before cutting and serving.

Serves 8 to 10.

DUNBAR HOUSE 1880
P.O. Box 1375
Murphys, California
95247
(209) 728-2897

No credit cards
Moderate

The Italiate Victorian historic Dunbar House is located in a gold rush town in the foothills of the Sierras.

Dunbar House 1880
Murphys, California

PETITE AUBERGE

Crustless Quiche

3 tablespoons butter
2 cups chopped vegetables
   (onions, green pepper,
   broccoli, cauliflower,
   asparagus or other as
   desired)
1 cup grated Swiss cheese

6 eggs
1½ cups heavy cream
½ teaspoon salt
¼ teaspoon pepper
pinch each of nutmeg and
   garlic powder
parmesan cheese to taste

Preheat over to 350°. Liberally butter a quiche dish.

Layer vegetables and Swiss cheese in dish halfway to the top.
Lightly beat together eggs, cream, salt, pepper and spices.
Pour over vegetables and cheese. Bake for 30 minutes,
Remove from oven, sprinkle parmesan cheese on top and
return to oven for 15 minutes more.

EAGLE HARBOR INN

Southwestern Eggs

1 green pepper, medium diced
½ red pepper, medium diced
1 small onion, finely diced
6 ounces Shitake mushrooms,
   sliced
6 eggs
1 cup heavy cream

¼ cup milk
dash of Tabasco Sauce
dash of thyme
dash of cumin
⅓ pound grated cheddar
   cheese

Preheat oven to 350 degrees.

Sauté green pepper, red pepper, onion, and Shitake mushrooms. Drain. Hold some aside for garnish. Beat eggs, heavy
cream, milk, Tabasco, thyme, and cumin. Add sauté to mixture. Grease two 6-inch pie tins and make a crust out of the
cheese. Pour egg mixture into pans.

Bake for 45 minutes. Garnish with sour cream and chili
powder.

Serves 12.

PETITE AUBERGE
863 Bush Street
San Francisco, California
94108
(415) 928-6000

MC/V/AE
Very expensive

The ambience of the French
countryside has found its
way to downtown San
Francisco. Petite Auberge,
with its 26 rooms, is filled
with antiques, flowers and
friendliness.

EAGLE HARBOR INN
9914 Water Street
Ephraim, Wisconsin
54211
(800) 324-5427
(414) 854-2121

MC/V
Moderate

An intimate New England-
styled country inn filled
with antiques and period
wallpapers. Located close to
boating, beaches, golf
course, and parks. Twelve
private cottages and queen-
size or double beds available.

ASA RANSOM HOUSE
Caraway and Sour Cream Soup

4 cups chicken stock
¼ cup chicken fat or ⅛ cup
    butter and ⅛ cup
    cooking oil
2 cups medium-dice onions
1 cup medium-dice celery
1 cup medium-dice carrots
salt and pepper
1 tablespoon caraway seeds
½ cup all-purpose flour
1 cup sour cream
½ cup milk

Heat the chicken stock. In a separate 3-quart saucepan, melt chicken fat or heat butter and oil mixture. Sauté onions, celery and carrots. Season lightly with salt and pepper. Add caraway seeds. Sauté until the onion is transparent. Reduce heat and add flour, stirring constantly so as not to scorch. Cook for 5 to 8 minutes to bind the flour and fat. Gradually add hot chicken stock, stirring to dissolve the roux (mixture of flour and fat). Bring the soup to a boil, then reduce heat and let simmer.

In a separate bowl, mix sour cream with one cup of hot soup and stir vigorously to prevent curdling. Pour this mixture back into the soup and heat, taking care not to allow soup to boil. Finally, add milk and season with salt and pepper to taste. Serve hot. Yields 2 quarts or servings for 8.

ASA RANSOM HOUSE
10529 Main Street
Clarence, New York
14031
(716) 759-2315

No credit cards
Moderate

This 4-room village inn includes a library, gift shop, tap-room and herb garden.

KENNISTON HILL INN

Cheese and Potato Pie

one 10-inch pie plate
4½ cups coarsely ground
   cheese (recommend a
   combination of cheddar,
   Swiss, and Monterey
   Jack)
1–2 tablespoons flour
1½ cups frozen shredded hash
   brown potato patty
   ½ inch dice
non-stick vegetable spray

1 tablespoon minced dry
   onion flakes
Marjoram
Parsley
4 eggs
1 cup half and half
1 teaspoon dry mustard
1 teaspoon Worcestershire
   sauce
Paprika

Preheat oven to 350 degrees. In a mixing bowl mix four cups of the cheese with the flour. Add the diced potato and mix. Spray pie plate with vegetable spray. Put half the cheese mixture in the pie plate. Lightly sprinkle onion on top. Cover with remaining cheese and potato mixture. Sprinkle marjoram and parsley on top. In a mixing bowl, whisk eggs together, add half and half, dry mustard, and Worcestershire sauce. Whisk ingredients together until frothy. Pour over cheese and potato mixture. Sprinkle remaining ½ cup of cheese on top, shake paprika on pie to finish.

Bake for 40–45 minutes. Let pie set thirty minutes before serving. Serve with fruit. Serves 6–8.

Kenniston Hill Inn, Boothbay Harbor, Maine

KENNISTON HILL INN
P.O. Box 125
Boothbay Harbor, Maine
04537
(800) 992-2915
(207) 633-2159

MC/V/AE
Moderate

The oldest inn in Boothbay Harbor (c. 1786) on four peaceful acres offering country antiques, fireplaces, and sitting rooms. Full country breakfasts, with diet restrictions accommodated.

THE COLUMNS

Eggplant St. Claire

cooking oil, enough for deep frying
1 cup all-purpose flour
egg wash (5 eggs beaten with small amount of water, a pinch of salt and pepper)
1 cup bread crumbs
4 eggplant halves, peeled and hollowed
2 ounces crabmeat, picked over
1 tablespoon heavy cream
pinch of seafood seasoning
minced garlic to taste
1 cup chopped parsley
1 pint heavy cream

1 pint oyster liquid (canned, if necessary)
chablis or other white wine, to taste
chicken base to taste
pinch of thyme
⅓ cup each of minced green onions, yellow onions, carrots, green bell peppers, celery and turnips
1 teaspoon Worcestershire Sauce
½ cup water
3 tablespoons cornstarch
8 oysters
4 peeled shrimp
chopped parsley for garnish

Fill deep fryer 5 to 6 inches deep with cooking oil. Preheat cooking oil to 320°.

Flour eggplant halves, dip in egg wash and roll in bread crumbs. Deep fry for 5 minutes, turning once. In a saucepan, mix together crabmeat, one tablespoon heavy cream, seafood seasoning (see following recipe), garlic and chopped parsley, and heat until hot. In another saucepan, bring 1 pint heavy cream and oyster liquid to a boil. Add white wine, chicken base, garlic, thyme, green onions, yellow onions, carrots, peppers, celery, turnips and Worcestershire Sauce and continue cooking over low heat. Add water to cornstarch to make a paste. Add cornstarch paste to oyster sauce, stirring over heat until sauce is thickened. Add oysters and shrimp to sauce. Remove from heat. Set deep-fried eggplant on individual plates. Fill each eggplant half with the hot crab filling and top with oyster sauce. Sprinkle with chopped parsley. Make sure each serving includes 2 oysters and 1 shrimp. Serves 4.

T H E   C O L U M N S

SEAFOOD SEASONING:

2½ ounces salt
1 ounce thyme
1 ounce oregano
¾ ounce black pepper

2 ounces paprika
2 ounces granulated garlic
½ ounce Cayenne papper

Combine all and store in a tightly covered container.

D O C K S I D E   G U E S T   Q U A R T E R S
Potato Salad

1½ pounds red potatoes
(about five medium size
potatoes)
2 tablespoons chopped parsley
2 tablespoons chopped fresh
dill or ¾ teaspoon dried
2 scallions, trimmed and
finely chopped

½ stalk of celery, chopped
2 tablespoons vinegar
1 cup mayonnaise
salt and freshly ground black
pepper

Put the potatoes in a large saucepan and cover with cold water. Bring to a boil and cook for 20–30 minutes, until potatoes are tender but still firm. Drain the potatoes and let cool slightly. Cut them into ½-inch pieces.

Put the potatoes in a large bowl and add parsley, dill, scallions, celery, vinegar, and mayonnaise. Season to taste with salt and pepper and toss gently to mix. Cover and chill until the flavors have had time to blend. Serves 6.

THE COLUMNS
Box 41
3811 Saint Charles Avenue
New Orleans, Louisiana
70115
(504) 899-9808

MC / V / AE
Expensive

Built in 1883 in the Garden District. The Columns has for years been one of New Orleans' finest small hotels and is listed in the National Register of Historic Places.

DOCKSIDE GUEST
QUARTERS
P.O. Box 205, Harris Island Road
York, Maine
03909
(207) 363-2868

MC/V
Moderate

Situated in an unsurpassed location along the edge of the harbor, this unique setting provides a tranquil and beautiful atmosphere. Rooms are tastefully decorated for warmth and comfort. AAA rated 3-diamonds.

THE INN AT MANCHESTER

Fresh Crab Casserole

1 pound fresh crab meat
½ teaspoon salt
½ teaspoon pepper
1 tablespoon chopped parsley
1 teaspoon minced onion
1 cup heavy cream or half-
and-half

1½ cups mayonnaise
4 hard-boiled eggs, cut in
chunks
2 slices homemade or good
quality white bread,
cubed

Preheat oven to 350°. Butter a casserole dish.

Combine first 8 ingredients. Put in casserole. Sprinkle cubes of bread over the top. Bake for 40 to 45 minutes. Serves 4.

Herbed Cream Cheese

1 clove garlic, mashed
8 ounces cream cheese
4 ounces whipped sweet
butter
⅛ teaspoon pepper

⅛ teaspoon thyme
⅛ teaspoon basil
⅛ teaspoon marjoram
⅛ teaspoon dill
¼ teaspoon oregano

Beat all ingredients together thoroughly. Chill 24 hours.

Remove from refrigerator to soften for easy spreading. Serve with crackers or bagel chips. Serves 4.

THE INN AT
MANCHESTER
Route 7A
Manchester Village,
Vermont
05254
(802) 362-1793

AE
Moderate

This 15-room inn is in the heart of a popular skiing area, and its swimming pool makes it a summer escape as well. The owner is also the chef.

The Inn at Manchester
Manchester Village, Vermont

BRACKENRIDGE HOUSE

Eggs and Artichokes

2 packages (9 ounces each)
    frozen artichoke hearts
    (or 2 cans artichoke hearts
    packed in water)
1 bay leaf
2 cans condensed cream of
    chicken soup

1 tablespoon chopped onion
¼ cup sherry
8 hard boiled eggs quartered
1–2 cups cheddar cheese,
    shredded
2 cups diced cooked ham

Preheat oven to 400 degrees.

Cook artichoke hearts as directed on package, adding bay leaf during cooking if desired. Drain. If using canned artichokes, drain thoroughly. Combine soup, onion and sherry. Mix well. Arrange artichoke hearts, eggs and ham in a 3-quart prepared casserole dish. Add soup mixture. Top with shredded cheese.

Bake for 25–30 minutes, or until cheese is lightly browned. May add meat dish on side.

Serves 8.

BRACKENRIDGE HOUSE
230 Madison
San Antonio, Texas
78204
(800) 221-1412
(210) 271-3442

Most Credit Cards
Expensive

A lovely blend of comfort and nostalgia, Brookhaven features high ceilings, wood floors, and fireplaces. Close to everything—the perfect getaway.

HALCYON PLACE

Crepes with Cheese Filling and Raspberry Sauce

HALCYON PLACE
197 Washington Street
Chemung/Elmira, New York
14825
(607) 529-3544

Most Credit Cards
Moderate

1825 Greek Revival home offers peace, tranquility and gracious hospitality for the discerning traveler. Period antiques abound. Full gourmet breakfasts including homemade herb cheese, lemon herb tea bread, and delicious cheese filled raspberry crepes. Relax and enjoy.

Crepes:
½ cup all-purpose flour
pinch salt
2 large eggs
1 egg yolk
1¼ cup milk
1 teaspoon vanilla
4 tablespoons butter

Filling:
1 pound ricotta cheese
1 egg, beaten
1 teaspoon sugar
⅛ teaspoon freshly grated
    nutmeg

Raspberry Sauce:
1 pint raspberries
1 teaspoon water
½ cup sugar (or to taste)
½ teaspoon grated orange zest

The crepes can be made the night before, filled, covered, and refrigerated until morning.

Crepes: Sift together flour and salt in a medium size bowl. Whisk in eggs, egg yolk and one tablespoon milk to form a smooth, paste-like batter. Add the rest of the milk and vanilla and mix well. There should be no lumps. Melt butter in a nonstick skillet and stir into batter leaving behind a film of butter in the skillet. Let batter rest at room temperature for thirty minutes. Heat skillet over medium-low heat. Stir batter and ladle about ¼ cup into pan. Thinly coat bottom and edges of pan with batter. Cook until crepe turns golden-grown, lacy, and begins to pull away from pan, approximately 2 minutes. Turn and cook other side 30 to 40 seconds. Slide from pan and continue cooking other crepes. Stack crepes on a plate.

Filling: Combine all filling ingredients in a bowl and blend well. Place a tablespoon of filling in the center of each crepe. Turn in opposite ends and roll up the crepes. Cover and refrigerate. In the morning, fry the crepes in three tablespoons butter in a large skillet over medium-high heat until golden.

Raspberry Sauce: Place half the raspberries in a saucepan with water and sugar. Cook over medium-high heat , stirring until sugar dissolves and sauce is thick. Add the remaining raspberries and orange zest. Heat through at the lowest temperature setting. Top filled crepes with raspberry sauce and garnish with sour cream and fresh raspberries. Serves 8.

CHALET SUZANNE

Shrimp Suzanne with Dill

½ cup sour cream
½ cup mayonnaise
½ cup chopped fresh
    cucumber, peeled and
    seeded
⅓ cup minced onion
1½ tablespoons fresh chopped
    dill
1% teaspoons lemon juice

garlic to taste
salt and appper
8 drops Tabasco
¼ teaspoon caraway seeds
1 pound shrimp (25 to 30
    count), cooked, peeled
    and cleaned
bibb lettuce

Mix first 10 ingredients together to make a sauce. Stir in shrimp. Mix well and chill. Serve on a bed of bibb lettuce, either as individual servings or in a lettuce-lined bowl.

Serves 4 to 6.

CHALET SUZANNE
P.O. Drawer AC
Lake Wales, Florida
33853
(941) 676-6011

All major credit cards
Expensive

With 30 rooms nestled on a private estate in central Florida, the Chalet Suzanne boasts its own lake, a swimming pool, private sirstrip and multi-award-winning restaurant.

GRAPEVINE INN

Spinach Crepes
with Eggs and Wild Mushrooms

GRAPEVINE INN
486 Siskiyou Boulevard
Ashland, Oregon
97520
(800) 500-VINE
(541) 482-7944

MC/V
Moderate

A romantic 1909 Dutch
Colonial inn. Rooms com-
plete with down comforters
and cozy fireplaces. Gourmet breakfasts are served in
the lush garden gazebo.
Nice walk to town and the-
atres.

1 cup flour
4 large eggs
1 teaspoon salt
¼ teaspoon ground black
    pepper
1½ cup milk
½ cup cooked chopped
    spinach
melted butter
2 tablespoons olive oil

1 cup coarsely chopped
    Portobello mushrooms
    (can combine with Shitake
    or Crimini Mushrooms)
2–3 tablespoons dry sherry
8–10 lightly beaten eggs
pepper to taste
3½ ounces blue cheese, crumbled
Sour cream

Preheat oven to 325 degrees. In blender, mix flour, eggs, salt, pepper and milk. Beat until well blended. Add spinach and pulse just to mix in. Heat crepe pan on medium-high heat and brush with melted butter. Pour ¼ cup batter in pan, swirl to coat pan and cook until bottom of crepe is lightly browned. Flip crepe over and cook other side briefly. Cool crepes completely.

In large frying pan, sauté mushrooms in olive oil, adding pepper and dry sherry. To mushroom mixture, add beaten eggs and scramble until set but still soft and glossy.

Taking ¼ cup mushroom/egg mixture, place down center of each crepe and roll up. Place rolls in greased pan, cover with foil and bake for 20–25 minutes until heated through. Serve crepes with sour cream and blue cheese on top. Serves 8.

Grapevine Inn, Ashland, Oregon

THE CROWN HOTEL

Dredge scampi in seasoned flour. Sauté in butter for one minute. Remove from pan and keep warm. Add mushrooms, tomatoes and onions to pan. Sauté for one minute. Stir in remaining ingredients and simmer for another minute. Return scampi to pan. Bring to a boil. Spoon over boiled rice. Serves 2.

PATCHWORK QUILT COUNTRY INN, INC.

Buttermilk Pecan Chicken

¾ cup (1½ sticks) butter
1 cup buttermilk
1 egg, lightly beaten
1 cup all-purpose flour
1 cup ground pecans
¼ cup sesame seeds
1 tablespoon paprika
1 tablespoon salt
⅛ teaspoon pepper
2 to 3½ pounds broiler-
  fryers, cut up
½ cup pecan halves

Preheat oven to 350°. Place butter in large shallow roasting pan and melt in oven. Remove and set aside.

In shallow dish mix buttermilk and egg. In medium bowl combine flour, ground pecans, sesame seeds, paprika, salt and pepper. Coat chicken in buttermilk mixture, then in flour mixture. Place in roasting pan, turning to coat all sides with butter, finishing with skin side up. Scatter pecan halves over chicken and bake about 1½ to 1¾ hours, until chicken is deep golden brown. Serves 8.

THE CROWN HOTEL
109 North Seminole Avenue
Inverness, Florida 32650
(904) 344–5555

V / AE / CB / DC
Expensive

The Crown Hotel began as a general store over a century ago and has evolved into a 34-room inn with swimming pool and award-winning restaurant.

PATCHWORK QUILT COUNTRY INN
11748 C.R. #2
Middlebury, Indiana 46540
(219) 825–2417

No credit cards
Moderate

Located in the heart of Amish country, this Hoosier country inn lives up to its name with patchwork quilts on all the beds.

BROWN-WILLIAMS HOUSE

Country Egg Casserole Soufflé

6 large eggs
2 cups grated Monterey and
    Colby jack cheeses
8 pre-browned link sausages,
    cut into slices
2 cups milk

2½ English muffins, cut into
    1 inch cubes
¾ teaspoon Dijon mustard
dash of cayenne pepper
fresh chive or scallion,
    chopped to taste

Preheat oven to 400 degrees.

Mix all ingredients together. Bake in a large glass baking dish for approximately 35 minutes, or until top is slightly browned and inserted knife comes out clean.

Serves 8.

BROWN-WILLIAMS
HOUSE
R.R. #1 Box 337 Rt. 28 North
Cooperstown, New York
13326
(607) 547-5569

Moderate

This 1825 Federal Inn is located on 4.5 acres of lawns and gardens. Hand-painted wall finishes, Shaker-Federal furnishings, breathtaking views, outdoor spa, and privacy awaits you at Brown-Williams House.

Brown-Williams House
Cooperstown, New York

M c C A L L U M   H O U S E

Italian Zucchini Quiche

4 cups thinly sliced zucchini
1 cup chopped green onion
*   with stems*
½ cup chopped parsley
1 teaspoon garlic salt
½ teaspoon pepper
¼ teaspoon basil

2 teaspoon gourmet mustard
¼ teaspoon oregano
2 cups shredded mozzarella
*   cheese (or Monterey jack)*
3 beaten eggs
non-stick cooking spray

Preheat oven to 375 degrees.

Sauté the sliced zucchini and chopped green onions using nonstick cooking spray for ten minutes. Stir in parsley, salt, pepper, basil, gourmet mustard, and oregano. Cool mixture. Then add and blend with mozzarella cheese (or Monterey jack) as well as eggs.

Pour into sprayed glass pie plate and bake for 25–30 minutes.

Serves 6–8.

McCALLUM HOUSE
613 W. 32nd
Austin, Texas
78705
(512) 451-6744

MC/V
Moderate

Explore beautiful Austin from this historic, antique-filled Victorian. Ten blocks from UT-Austin, 20 blocks from the Capitol and downtown.

STEAMBOAT INN

Sharon Van Loan's
Cold Salmon with Mustard Sauce

5 to 10 pounds cleaned whole fresh salmon (For fish with head and tail, allow about 1 pound per person.)
2 tablespoons lemon juice
¾ cup mayonnaise
3 to 4 stalks celery with leaves, chopped

3 to 4 onion slices
garnishes of lemon wedges, cucumber slices and parsley sprigs
mustard sauce (see following recipe)

Preheat oven to 450°. Oil a large piece of heavy foil.

Rinse and pat salmon dry. Allow to stand at room temperature for 1½ to 2 hours. Blend lemon juice into mayonnaise. Combine mixture with celery and onion and put into the cavity of the fish. Wrap the fish in the oiled foil, place on a large cookie sheet and bake for 10 to 12 minutes per pound, or until the flesh along the backbone is just beginning to lose its translucence. Turn fish over about halfway through baking time. When done, unwrap foil to release steam and allow salmon to cool. Remove skin from exposed side of fish and gently scrape brown matter (nerve and fat tissue) away. Spoon out mayonnaise stuffing and place fish on serving platter surrounded by stuffing. Decorate with lemon wedges, cucumber slices and lots of parsley. Serve with mustard sauce (see following recipe). Serves 6 to 8.

MUSTARD SAUCE:

2 egg yolks
2 tablespoons Dijon mustard
1½ teaspoons dry mustard
1 teaspoon salt
dash of Cayenne pepper
2 teaspoons tarragon vinegar

¾ cup vegetable oil
1 tablespoon chopped shallots
1 tablespoon sour cream
¼ teaspoon Bovril™ bouillon, dissolved in 1 tablespoon warm water
3 tablespoons heavy cream

S T E A M B O A T I N N

Put yolks, mustards, salt and Cayenne into blender jar and blend until very thick. Blend in vinegar. Slowly add vege table oil with blender running. When thick and well mixed, add shallots, sour cream, dissolved bouillon and cream. Blend and store in refrigerator until ready to use. (May be made up to several days in advance and kept in the refrigerator.)

This amount is adequate for a small fish. For a 10-pound fish, double the recipe.

W O O D L A N D I N N B & B

Frank's Seafood Omelet

8 green onions, chopped
2 cups fresh mushrooms,
　sliced
1 dozen medium size shrimp
　(cooked and halved
　lengthwise)
8 ounces crab meat (cooked or
　imitation)

½ cup sour cream
8 eggs (2 per omelet)
1–2 cups grated Swiss cheese
2 tablespoons butter or
　margarine

Sauté onions and mushrooms in butter or margarine until soft. Add seafood and add sour cream, stir together and warm over very low temperature and set aside. (Sour cream should not boil.)

Whip eggs (two at a time) and pour into a buttered 8-inch omelet pan over medium to high heat. Lift edges frequently to allow uncooked portion to flow underneath. Sprinkle ¼ to ½ cup of cheese over center portion of omelet. Cover and cook 1 to 2 minutes at medium temperature. Add ½ cup of seafood mixture on the top of one half of the omelet. Cover and cook until egg mixture is set (approximately 2 minutes).

Fold omelet over seafood portion, slide onto a warm plate, garnish top with halved shrimp and a sprig of parsley. Serve with fresh fruit and hot muffins or sliced bread.

Serves 4.

STEAMBOAT INN
42705 North Umpqua
Highway
Steamboat, Oregon
(800) 840-8825
(541) 498-2411

MC/V
Moderate

On the Umpqua River in the Cascade Mountains, this favorite Oregon fishing lodge is famous for its hearty fishermen's dinners.

WOODLAND INN B&B
159 Trull Road
Woodland Park, Colorado
80863
(800) 226-9565
(719) 687-8209

Most Credit Cards
Moderate

This secluded, romantic retreat is nestled on twelve acres of aspen and fir trees, with breathtaking views of Pikes Peak. Relaxation and comfort abound. Hot air balloon rides available.

SHELTER HARBOR INN

Creamed Lobster and Johnnycakes

4 tablespoons butter
1 teaspoon finely minced
    shallots
4 tablespoons all-purpose
    flour
1 cup fish stock (or bottled
    clam juice), hot
¼ cup Madeira
1 cup heavy cream
⅛ teaspoon nutmeg

⅛ teaspoon salt
⅛ teaspoon freshly ground
    pepper
⅛ teaspoon Cayenne pepper
2 cups lobster meat
    (reserving whole claw
    meat for garnish)
12 johnnycakes (see
    following recipe)

Melt butter in a heavy saucepan. Add shallots and sauté over moderate heat until tender. Stir in flour and cook, stirring constantly for about 2 minutes, without browning. Remove from heat and stir in the hot stock gradually. Return to heat and stir with a wire whisk until smooth and thick. Stir in Madeira and then heavy cream. Season with nutmeg, salt, pepper and Cayenne. Fold in lobster meat (except for reserved claw). Serve creamed lobster over 3 johnnycakes and garnish with claw. Serves 4 to 6.

SHELTER HARBOR INN JOHNNYCAKES:

2 cups white cornmeal
1½ teaspoons salt
2 teaspoons sugar
2 cups boiling water
½ cup milk, scalded
    and still hot

1 egg, lightly beaten
½ cup bacon fat or other
    cooking oil (enough to
    keep griddle greased)

Mix cornmeal, salt and sugar. Add boiling water and milk and mix well. Stir in egg. Drop by tablespoon onto a medium hot, well-greased griddle or heavy frying pan and fry for 5 minutes on each side. Makes 16 to 20 johnnycakes. Serves 4 to 6.

SHELTER HARBOR INN
10 Wagner Road
Route 1
Westerly, Rhode Island
02891
(401) 322–8883

MC / V / AE
Moderate

This 18-room 18th-century farmhouse-turned-B & B inn is noted for its country cooking.

THE LONE MOUNTAIN RANCH

Dill Bread

2 tablespoons active dry
    yeast
½ cup lukewarm water
4 tablespoons minced fresh
    dill weed
2 tablespoons butter
2 cups cottage cheese

4 tablespoons brown sugar
2 tablespoons minced onion
2 teaspoons salt
½ teaspoon baking soda
2 eggs
4½ cups all-purpose flour

Combine yeast and lukewarm water and set aside. Mix together dill and butter. Combine the remaining ingredients to form dough. After the yeast has begun to bubble, work it into the dough, along with the dill butter. Mix in cottage cheese, brown sugar, onion, salt and baking soda mixture. Knead in flour. Knead for 5 minutes or until gluten forms. The dough should be sticky. Allow it to rise until double in size. Punch down. Allow it to rise again until double in size. Preheat oven to 350°. Punch down dough and roll out. Form into 2 loaves. Bake for about 40 to 45 minutes until golden brown. When done, bread will sound hollow when mittened fist is thumped on bottom of pan. Yields 2 loaves, which each yield 16 slices.

LONE MOUNTAIN
RANCH
P.O. BOX 160069
Big Sky, Montana
59716
(406) 995–4644

MC / V / AE
Expensive

These log cabins near Yellowstone National Park are a family favorite for a summer ranch experience or winter ski vacation.

Lone Mountain Ranch
Big Sky, Montana

INN AT CEDAR FALLS

Potato & Scallion Soufflés

4 eggs
1 tablespoon fresh diced
   scallion
½ cup cooked shredded potato
2 tablespoons milk

1 teaspoon baking powder
¼ cup shredded cheddar
   cheese
salt and pepper to taste

Preheat oven to 350 degrees.

Butter four glass ramekins (little glass fruit cups). Mix all ingredients in a bowl. Season with salt and pepper.

Bake for 15–25 minutes or until tops are lightly browned and centers are firm. Serve in the glass cup. Warn guests that the cups are quite hot.

Serves 4.

INN AT CEDAR FALLS
21190 St. Rt. 374
Logan, Ohio
43138
(614) 385-7489

MC/V
Moderate

Rooms in this 1840's log cabin are furnished with antiques and abundant in charm. Gourmet meals are prepared from the inn's organic garden. The sitting room and library are the perfect rest spot after a day of hiking in the surrounding Hocking State Park.

Inn at Cedar Falls
Logan, Ohio

SALISBURY HOUSE

Baked Blintz

Filling:
1 six ounce package cream
    cheese (room temperature)
1 cup low-fat cottage cheese
1 egg beaten
1 tablespoon sugar
1 teaspoon vanilla

Batter:
½ cup butter or margarine
    (room temperature)
⅓ cup sugar
4 eggs
1 cup flour
2 teaspoons baking powder
1 cup plain yogurt
½ cup low-fat sour cream
½ cup orange juice

Preheat oven to 375 degrees. Butter and flour a 9 by 13 inch casserole dish. In a small bowl, beat cream cheese, add cottage cheese, egg, sugar, and vanilla, mix well and set aside.

In a large bowl, cream butter and sugar. Add eggs one at a time beating well. Add flour and baking powder. Mix in sour cream and yogurt and add orange juice.

Pour ½ of batter into prepared casserole dish, layer in filling and then top with remaining batter. Bake 45–50 minutes until lightly browned. Slice into squares and serve with a dollop of sour cream or yogurt and fresh berry preserves. Serves 8.

SALISBURY HOUSE
750 16th Avenue East
Seattle, Washington
98112
(206) 328-8682

Most Credit Cards
Moderate

This elegant Capitol Hill home is ideally located for business or pleasure. Take advantage of Seattle's excellent transit system. Only minutes to downtown, the University of Washington, and Seattle University.

Salisbury House
Seattle, Washington

THE VENICE BEACH HOUSE

Elaine's Apple Dumplings

2 cups all-purpose flour
1 teaspoon salt
2 teaspoons baking powder
12 tablespoons (1½ sticks) chilled butter
½ cup milk
2 cups sugar
2 cups water
¼ teaspoon cinnamon
¼ teaspoon nutmeg
4 tablespoons butter

6 or 8 small apples, cored but not skinned
½ cup brown sugar
½ cup raisins and chopped nuts, combined
½ cup granola
1 teaspoon cinnamon
3 or 4 teaspoons butter
1 cup or more sour cream, to taste

To prepare the pastry, sift together flour, salt and baking powder. Cut in the chilled butter, add milk and stir just long enough to moisten the flour. Roll dough out on floured board to ¼" thickness and allow to rest for at least ½ hour.

Meanwhile, prepare a syrup of the sugar, water and spices. Simmer for 5 minutes, then add 4 tablespoons butter. Set aside.

Preheat oven to 275°. Butter a jelly roll pan.

Peel and partially core apples, to create a cavity, but do not cut through bottom. Cut pastry into 5" squares (depending on size of apple), and place one apple on each square. Fill the cavity with a mixture of brown sugar, raisins, nuts and cinnamon, and dot with ½ teaspoon butter. Fold corners and pinch all edges together. Repeat with remaining apples. Place one inch apart on the jelly roll pan. Pour syrup over the "dumplings." Bake for 35 minutes. Serve with sour cream. Serves 6 to 8.

THE VENICE
BEACH HOUSE
15 30th Avenue
Venice, California
90291
(310) 823-1966

MC / V / AE
Expensive

An 8-room historic land-
mark, The Venice Beach
House is not far from the
beach and other attractions
of this unusual Los Angeles
community.

THE GRISWOLD INN
Monte Carlo Sandwiches

8 ounces sliced turkey
12 slices white bread, thickly
    buttered (use softened
    butter)

8 ounces sliced ham
4 ounces sliced Swiss cheese
8 eggs, lightly beaten
6 ounces butter

Preheat oven to 350°.

Place ¼ of the sliced turkey on top of one slice of buttered
bread. On another slice, put ¼ of the sliced ham and ¼ of
the sliced Swiss cheese. Stack the ham and cheese layer on
top of the turkey layer. Place the last slice of bread on top
(bread will be on the top, in the middle and on the bottom).
Repeat with remaining bread, meats and cheese. Cut crust
off and cut in half. Wrap sandwiches in plastic wrap and
refrigerate until butter has hardened. Dip sandwiches into
beaten egg. Melt some butter in a sauté pan and sauté
sandwiches a few at a time until browned on both sides. Place
in oven and bake for 10 minutes. Serves 4.

BED & BREAKFAST HAWAII
Papaya Seed Dressing

1 teaspoon salt
½ cup sugar
1½ teaspoons dry mustard
1 cup red wine vinegar
2 cups salad oil

2 tablespoons papaya seeds
½ cup chopped macadamia
    nuts
½ onion, minced

In a blender, mix salt, sugar, mustard and vinegar. Add oil
gradually with blender running. Remove to a serving bowl.
In blender, blend together papaya seeds, macadamia nuts and
onion. Stir into oil and vinegar mixture. Best served chilled
over any type of tossed greens. Serves 6 or more.

GRISWOLD INN
36 Main Street
Essex, Connecticut
06426
(860) 767-1776

MC/V/AE/DC
Expensive

Located in a riverside town,
the Griswold Inn has been
in operation for 207 years.

BED & BREAKFAST
HAWAII
P.O. Box 449
Kapaa, Hawaii
96746
(808) 822-7771

No credit cards
Inexpensive to moderate

This is one of Hawaii's two
B & B reservation service
organizations, which place
visitors in private guest
houses.

GARRATT MANSION
Herbal Popovers

GARRATT MANSION
900 Union Street
Alameda, California
94501
(510) 521-4779

No credit cards
Moderate

In this quiet San Francisco island suburb, guests can bicycle to the beach, observe the harbor life, or stroll down Alameda's shady streets.

3 eggs
1 cup milk
1 cup all-purpose flour
3 tablespoons butter, melted

1 teaspoon dried thyme, sage
    or crushed basil
½ teaspoon celery salt

Preheat oven to 450°. Butter eight 6-ounce custard cups.

In blender container, mix eggs, milk, flour, butter, herbs and celery salt. Cover and process at low speed until just smooth. Spoon about ⅓ cup of the batter into each custard cup. Bake for 15 minutes. Reduce heat to 375° and bake for 30 minutes longer or until browned. Serve immediately. Serves 4.

*Garratt Mansion
Alameda, California*

E D W A R D I A N   I N N

Edwardian Buns

5 to 6 cups all-purpose
　　flour
1 cup sugar
2 packages active dry yeast
1 teaspoon salt
¾ cup water

½ cup butter
2 eggs
½ cup cooked mashed
　　potatoes
⅛ teaspoon ground nutmeg
melted butter

Combine 1 cup flour sugar, yeast and salt in a large mixing bowl. Stir well. Heat water and butter in a small saucepan (temperature should reach 115° to 120°). Gradually add hot mixture to flour mixture, beating at low speed with an electric mixer until combined. Beat 2 minutes more at medium speed. Beat in eggs, potato, nutmeg and ¾ cup flour and continue beating for an additional 2 minutes. Gradually stir in enough of the remaining flour to make a soft dough. Turn dough out onto a well-floured surface and knead until smooth and elastic (about 10 minutes). Shape into a ball and place in a well-buttered bowl, turning the dough to cover with butter. Cover and allow to rise in a warm, draft-free place for 1½ hours. Punch down and let rise once more, until double in bulk. Divide dough into 12 equal parts. Roll each into a ball and place on buttered baking sheet. Press balls lightly with fingertips to shape them into buns. Cover and allow to rise until double. Brush buns with melted butter. Bake at 375° for 15 to 20 minutes or until golden. Remove immediately. Yields 12.

EDWARDIAN INN
317 Biscoe
Helena, Arkansas
72342
(501) 338–9155

MC / V / AE
Moderate

This antique-appointed 112-room inn evokes the feeling of life in a Mississippi River town at the turn of the century.

LOGWOOD INN

Aunt Margaret's
Pennsylvania Dutch Sticky Buns

1 package active dry yeast
2 cups warm water
    (130°F)
2 tablespoons sugar
5½ to 6 cups all-purpose
    flour
1 egg, beaten
1 teaspoon salt

⅓ cup sugar
1 stick (4 ounces) butter,
    softened
1 cup butter, softened
2 tablespoons sugar
1 teaspoon cinnamon
1½ cup syrup of choice
1 cup walnuts

In a large bowl, dissolve yeast in the warm water and stir until dissolved. Add sugar and 2 cups flour. Beat until smooth. Allow this mixture to stand for 15 to 20 minutes. With a spoon, add the egg, salt, sugar and 4 ounces softened butter. Gradually mix in the remaining flour. Cover with a towel, and allow dough to rise for 1 to 1½ hours in a warm spot. Roll out the dough on a floured board until it is a 15" by 24" rectangle. Spread it with 1 cup softened butter, and sprinkle sugar and cinnamon over the top. Roll the dough rectangle lengthwise, and slice it into 1" slices. Place slices side-by-side into pans which have been buttered and lined with syrup and walnuts. Allow buns to rise another hour. Bake in preheated 400° oven until nicely browned. Makes 12 to 15 buns.

Anadama Bread

According to legend, this delicious bread was invented by an early American fisherman whose wife did not bake. He named his creation after her: Anna, damn her.

7½ to 8½ cups unsifted all-
    purpose flour
2¾ teaspoon salt
2 packages active dry yeast
½ cup butter, softened

2¾ cups warm water
    (130°F)
¾ cup molasses
1¼ cups cornmeal

WALK-ABOUT CREEK

Combine about 2½ cups flour with salt and yeast. Stir in softened butter. Add water and molasses slowly, blending well. Beat at medium speed with an electric mixer for 2 minutes. Stir in ½ cup flour, and beat at high speed for 2 minutes more. Stir in cornmeal and enough additional flour to form a stiff dough. Turn out onto a floured board and knead until smooth and elastic (about 10 minutes). Place in a large buttered bowl, and butter the top of the dough. Cover and allow it to rise in a warm place until double in bulk (about one hour). Punch down and divide into two parts. Shape dough into 14" by 9" rectangles. Roll the dough up from it short upper end, and seal the sides, folding the sealed end over and pressing them closed. Place loaves with seam side down in 2 buttered loaf pans. Cover with a towel, and allow them to rise until double in bulk (about 45 minutes). Bake in a preheated oven set at 375 degrees for 40 to 45 minutes or until the loaves sound hollow when tapped. Remove from the pans, and cool on a wire rack. Loaves freeze well.

1801 INN

Auntie Hazel's Bread Pudding

5 cups crumbled, left-over bread, muffins, and/or cake
4 cups buttermilk
1 cup currants, raisins, cranberries or dried cherries
zest of 2 lemons or 1 orange

6 eggs (well beaten)
3 egg whites beaten till peaks form
1 teaspoon vanilla
butter (optional)
1 cup brown sugar
2 teaspoons cinnamon

Preheat oven to 350 degrees. Crumble bread or muffins. Soak in buttermilk to cover. Use food processor or ricer to even out the texture. Add dried fruit and lemon or orange zest. Add well-beaten eggs. Fold in beaten egg whites to lighten the mixture. Add vanilla. Top with butter, brown sugar, and cinnamon.

Bake until a knife inserted in the center comes out clean. Recommend serving with lemon yogurt or warmed marmalade. Serves 8

WALK-ABOUT CREEK
199 Edson Hill Road
Stowe, Vermont
05672
(802) 253-7354
(800) 426-6697

MC/V/AE
Moderate

Located beside a mountain stream, this quiet, peaceful establishment is a year-round getaway, with swimming pool and tennis courts, and Stowe's famed ski slopes nearby.

1801 INN
1801 First Street
Napa, California
94559
(707) 224-3739

Most Credit Cards
Expensive

This lovely, restored Queen Anne style Victorian home is located at the gateway to the famous Napa Wine Country. Each suite is appointed with a king size bed, fireplace and private bath. Heady scents of wine float through the air.

DIE HEIMAT COUNTRY INN

Sauerkraut

2 medium-size heads of
   cabbage

1 teaspoon sugar
2 tablespoons salt

Mix all ingredients thoroughly in a large bowl. Shred then mash cabbage with potato masher until juice collects. Cover bowl with cloth, and let stand for 2 hours. Press kraut into 3 sterilized quart jars as firmly as possible, then fill with the liquid collected in bowl. Fit screw tops loosely so that the kraut can ferment. Let stand at room temperature for several days. Press down again, and if necessary, make a weak salt solution (about 1½ cups salt to one quart water) to fill jars with liquid. Screw tops on tightly and store in a cool place. Sauerkraut is ready to use in 4 weeks. It may be eaten raw as a relish, just as it comes from the jar, or cooked.

Cooked Sauerkraut and Potato

2 cups cooked sauerkraut

1 medium raw potato, grated

Add potato to sauerkraut, cook 10 minutes, and serve.

*Die Heimat Country Inn
Homestead, Iowa*

DIE HEIMAT COUNTRY INN
Plain Cooked Sauerkraut

2 cups sauerkraut   caraway seed (optional)
2 tablespoons lard   water to cover

Cook all together for 15 minutes and serve.

OLD LOUISVILLE INN
Apple Bacon Chutney

¾ cup apple cider vinegar   3 tart green apples, peeled,
½ cup apple cider   cored and diced
1½ cups brown sugar   ¼ cup fresh orange juice
1½ cups diced smoked bacon

In a large saucepan, combine the vinegar, cider and brown sugar. Cook over high heat until bubbly, stir the first 30 seconds to dissolve sugar. Turn down heat to medium and continue to cook for 15 minutes.

In a small skillet, cook the diced bacon over medium heat until crisp. Drain bacon. Add bacon, apples and orange juice to the vinegar mixture. Return to boil and cook for 30 minutes more. Serve warm over waffles or pancakes. Makes 2 cups.

Old Louisville Inn, Louisville, Kentucky

DIE HEIMAT COUNTRY INN
Homestead, Iowa 52236
(319) 622-3937

MC/V
Inexpensive

This century-old, 19-room inn is in the middle of Iowa's historic Amana colonies.

OLD LOUISVILLE INN
1359 South Third Street
Louisville, Kentucky 40280
(502) 635-1574

MC/V
Moderate

"Your home away from home." Wake up to the aroma of freshly baked breads, muffins, and Southern hospitality. Children under 12 are free.

THE VOSS INN B & B

Sticky Buns

½ cup sugar
6 cups unsifted all-purpose
    flour
1½ teaspoons salt
2 packages active dry yeast
1 cup milk
⅔ cup water
¼ cup butter
2 eggs, at room temperature

¾ cup melted butter
    (approximately)
½ cup brown sugar
    (approximately)
⅓ teaspoon cinnamon
    (approximately)
¼ cup white sugar
    (approximately)
¼ cup peanut oil
    (approximately)

Spray 4 round cake pans with Pam vegetable cooking spray. Mix 5 cups flour, sugar, salt and yeast. Heat to lukewarm the milk, water and ½ cup butter, and mix them into the flour mixture. Add eggs, working into a dough with your hands (or use the dough hook of an electric mixer). Slowly add last cup of flour. Turn onto a board and knead for 10 minutes. Allow dough to rise in a greased bowl for 20 to 30 minutes. Punch down on a lightly-floured board and roll into a rectangle. Melt the remaining butter. Using a little more than half of the melted butter, cover the bottoms of the 4 round cake pans. Pour the rest of the butter over the dough rectangle, spreading to cover. Sprinkle brown sugar over butter in pans and over the dough rectangle. Combine cinnamon and white sugar and sprinkle over the dough, roll it up, and slice into 24 buns. Place 6 buns in each pan and brush tops with peanut oil. Refrigerate, covered, for 2 to 24 hours.

Preheat oven to 375°. Allow buns to stand at room temperature for 20 to 30 minutes, then bake 25 minutes or until done. Yields 24 sticky buns.

THE VOSS INN
BED & BREAKFAST
319 South Wilson
Bozeman, Montana
59715
(406) 587-0982

MC/V
Moderate

This 100-year-old red brick mansion lies in the heart of the university town of Bozeman. Each of its 6 guest rooms has a restored brass or iron bed and a unique personality.

F R I E N D S   L A K E   I N N

Baked Apples
Stuffed with Atateka Pudding

4 cups milk
⅓ cup cornmeal
¾ cup dark molasses
¼ cup butter
1 teaspoon salt
1 teaspoon ginger

½ teaspoon cinnamon
3 tablespoons sugar
1 egg, well beaten
8 apples, Granny Smith
  preferably

Preheat oven to 325 degrees. In the top of a double boiler scald the milk and stir in cornmeal. Place over boiling water and cook for 15 minutes. Stir in the molasses and cook for another 5 minutes. Remove from the heat and stir in butter, salt, ginger, cinnamon, sugar and egg. Pour the batter into a well greased baking dish.

Bake in oven for 1½ to 2 hours. Remove from oven and allow to stand 10–15 minutes. Core and scoop center of apples. With ice cream scoop, fill apples with pudding and bake in oven for 15 minutes. Serve warm with vanilla ice cream.

Serves 8.

Friends Lake Inn
Chestertown, New York

FRIENDS LAKE INN
Friends Lake Road
Chestertown, New York
12817
(518) 494-4751

MC/V
Expensive

A fully restored 19th century inn with beautiful lake view. Award-wining restaurant and wine list. 14 romantic guest rooms, cross-country skiing and mountain biking. Jacuzzis available in some rooms.

GREENVILLE ARMS, 1889

Moravian Orange Rolls

5 to 6 cups unsifted
   all-purpose flour
⅔ cup sugar
1 teaspoon salt
2 packages active
   dry yeast
⅓ cup softened butter
1 cup warm water
   (120° to 130°F)

1 cup mashed potatoes at
   room temperature
2 eggs at room temperature
½ cup softened butter
2 cups firmly packed light
   brown sugar
2 tablespoons orange juice
1 teaspoon ground cinnamon
1 teaspoon grated orange peel

In a large bowl, thoroughly mix 1½ cups flour, sugar, salt and yeast. Stir in ⅓ cup softened butter. Gradually add warm water and beat 2 minutes with an electric mixer at medium speed. Add potatoes, eggs and ½ cup flour. Beat well. Stir in enough additional flour to make a soft dough. Turn out onto lightly-floured board. Knead for 8 to 10 minutes. Place in a greased bowl, turning to grease the top. Cover and allow dough to rise in a warm, draft-free place until doubled in bulk (about one hour).

Greenville Arms
Greenville, New York

GREENVILLE ARMS, 1889

Meanwhile, cream ½ cup butter with brown sugar. Blend in orange juice, cinnamon and orange peel. When doubled, punch down dough. Turn out onto lightly-floured board and divide in half. Roll half of the dough into a 12" by 18" rectangle. Spread with half the sugar mixture and roll up like a jelly roll. Seal edges firmly. Slice into 18 equal pieces. Repeat with remaining dough and sugar mixture. Arrange on edge in 4 staggered rows of 9 slices in a buttered 9" pan. Allow rolls to rise about one hour until they have doubled in size.

Bake at 350° about 30 minutes or until done. Cool on wire racks. Yields 36 rolls.

AUNT ABIGAIL'S B & B INN

Berry Bundt Cake

1½ cups sifted cake flour
   (not self-rising)
1½ teaspoon baking soda
3 tablespoons instant dry
   nonfat milk
½ teaspoon salt
1 teaspoon cinnamon
½ teaspoon nutmeg
½ teaspoon cloves

½ cup oat bran
½ cup chopped almonds
1½ cups sugar
¾ cup plain yogurt
   (low fat)
3 eggs (beaten)
¾ cup corn oil
½ teaspoon orange extract
1 cup berries of your choice

Preheat oven to 350°. Grease and flour a 12-cup Bundt pan. Mix together the first eight ingredients. Mix in chopped nuts.

In a separate bowl, mix sugar and yogurt. Beat in eggs, corn oil and orange extract. Fold in berries.

Combine wet and dry ingredients, stirring just enough to blend. Pour into prepared Bundt pan. Bake 45–50 minutes. Cool 15 minutes. Serves 12.

GREENVILLE ARMS, 1889
P.O. Box 659
Greenville, New York
12083
(518) 966-5219

No credit cards
Expensive

The former home of William Vanderbilt in the foothills of the Catskills, the Greenville Arms offers 7 acres of lush lawn, a quaint stream and bridges, gardens and swimming pools for a relaxing weekend getaway.

AUNT ABIGAIL'S B & B INN
2120 "G" Street
Sacramento, California
95816
(916) 441-5007

Moderate

Ideal for business travelers and romantic escapes, this grand old mansion is in the heart of the State Capitol. Wonderful baked goods and vegetarian food are available. Enjoy!

CARTER HOUSE
Baked Pears Caramel

6 pears

Cut pears in half and core.

Make 4 to 5 slices in pear halves, being careful not to cut all the way through. Butter pan; place pear halves in pan and broil, not too close to flames, for 5 minutes.

SAUCE:

⅔ cup sugar
3 tablespoons cold water
3 tablespoons hot water

1½ cups whipping cream
1 teaspoon vanilla
1 teaspoon well-chilled unsalted butter

Cook sugar and cold water in sauce pan until sugar melts. Low heat.

Increase heat and bring to boil, brushing sides of pan with wet pastry brush. Boil until syrup becomes light brown. Remove from heat and add hot water. Add cream. Return pan to burner on medium heat and boil until sauce thickens; then add vanilla and butter.

Pour 2 to 3 tablespoons of sauce onto a small, preferably white, dish. Place pear half on top of sauce. Garnish with a mint leaf. Serves 6.

CARTER HOUSE
301 "L" Street
Eureka, California
95501
(800) 444-8062

V / AE / MC
Moderate

The Carter House is a newly built Victorian. The food is truly special. Sumptuous breakfasts are served in a lovely dining room. Let the cordials or tea and cookies send you off to sweet dreams!

R O M E O   I N N

Beer Bagels

2 tablespoons active dry
  yeast
one 12-ounce can of
  beer, at room tem-
  perature

3 tablespoons sugar
1 tablespoon salt
4½ cups all-purpose flour
cornmeal (enough to dust a
  baking sheet)

Dissolve yeast in ½ cup lukewarm beer. Combine remaining beer with sugar and salt. Stir until sugar is dissolved, then add 1 cup flour and yeast mixture. Stir in 3 cups flour to make a stiff dough and knead until smooth (approximately 10 minutes). Cover and let rise in a warm, draft-free place for one hour.

Preheat oven to 375°. Divide dough into 10 pieces and let it relax for 3 minutes. Bring 2 quarts water and 1 tablespoon sugar to a boil. Reduce heat and let simmer. Shape balls into bagels and allow to rest for 10 minutes. Drop bagels into simmering water, 2 or 3 at a time, for 45 seconds, turning once. Remove from water and drain on towel. Place on nonstick baking sheet sprinkled with cornmeal and bake for 30 minutes. Yields 10 bagels.

ROMEO INN
295 Idaho Street
Ashland, Oregon
97520
(503) 488-0884

No credit cards
Expensive

A large, comfortable guest house with swimming pool, hot tub and afternoon tea, the Romeo Inn is within walking distance of Ashland's Shakespeare Festival Theater.

Romeo Inn
Ashland, Oregon

GOLDEN RULE B & B

Cherry Coffee Cake

1½ cup flour
½ cup sugar
½ teaspoon baking soda
½ teaspoon baking powder
½ teaspoon salt
½ cup butter
½ cup buttermilk
1 egg, lightly beaten

½ teaspoon vanilla
1 cup cherry pie filling

Crumb Topping:
⅓ cup sugar
¼ cup flour
2 tablespoons butter

Preheat oven to 350 degrees. Grease and flour an 8-inch spring-form pan. Combine 1½ cups flour, ½ cup sugar, baking soda, baking powder, and salt. With a pastry blender, cut in ½ cup butter until pieces are the size of small peas. Set aside.

In a separate bowl combine buttermilk, egg, and vanilla. Pour wet ingredients into dry ingredients and blend. Do not over beat. Spread ⅔ of the batter into a pan. Spoon cherry pie filling evenly over dough. Spoon remaining batter over pie filling.

To make crumb topping, combine remaining ⅓ cup sugar and ¼ cup flour. With a pastry blender, cut in 2 tablespoons butter. Sprinkle over top of dough.

Bake for 45–50 minutes or until a toothpick inserted in center of cake comes out clean. Cool cake in pan on wire rack. Remove from pan before serving. Serves 8.

GOLDEN RULE B&B
6934 Rice Road
Victor, New York
14564
(716) 924-0610

Moderate

A uniquely renovated and enlarged 1865 country schoolhouse furnished with many antiques. Afternoon tea served in picnic area, sitting room, or hammock. Sumptuous, gourmet breakfasts every morning; candlelight breakfasts available upon request.

Golden Rule B&B, Victor, New York

E I L E R ' S   I N N

Place the apples in a row, front to back, on the far right side of the phyllo. Using the towel to help, roll the dough and apples towards the left. Place on a baking sheet and butter the strudel roll well. Bake for about 25 minutes or until golden in color. Place the baked strudel on a board, and slice into pieces. Sift powdered sugar over the roll. Serve with whipped cream laced with cognac vanilla* and sweetened with powdered sugar. Serves 8.

*Kay Tripp of Eiler's Inn prepares her own vanilla by soaking 10 vanilla beans (sliced and scraped) and seeds in a bottle of "the best quality cognac you are willing to buy." The bottle is turned each day and matures in a couple of weeks. As the contents of the bottle dwindle, the mixture can be extended with more beans and cognac.

EILER'S INN
741 South Coast Highway
Laguna Beach, California
92651
(714) 494-3004

MC/V/AE
Very expensive

This inn, built around a courtyard, serves breakfast and afternoon wine and cheese around a fountain.

O A K   S Q U A R E

Old Fashioned Syllabub

Syllabub was served in colonial days as ice cream is now, and is frequently found in cookbooks of the early 18th century.

1½ cups milk
3 eggs
¾ cup sugar

½ teaspoon salt
3 cups light cream
2 cups sweet wine

Scald milk. Beat eggs and add sugar and salt. Gradually mix hot milk into egg mixture and cook over hot water, stirring constantly, until mixture thickens. Cool. Add the light cream and wine and refrigerate. Serve cold in custard cups or glasses. Makes enough for 4 to 6 servings.

OAK SQUARE
1207 Church Street
Port Gibson, Mississippi
39150
(601) 437-4350

MC/V/AE
Expensive

Listed on the National Register of Historic Places, Oak Square is a palatial mansion in a town said by General U.S. Grant to be too beautiful to burn.

HOLLILEIF B & B

Zucchini Muffins

2 large eggs, beaten
¾ cup sugar
⅜ cup oil
1½ cups shredded zucchini
1⅛ cups flour
⅜ teaspoon baking soda

⅜ teaspoon baking powder
⅜ teaspoon salt
⅜ teaspoon nutmeg
⅜ cup chopped dates
⅜ cup chopped walnuts

Preheat oven to 350 degrees.

Beat eggs. Add sugar and oil. Beat 30 seconds and set aside. Stir in zucchini. Sift dry ingredients into bowl. Add egg mixture, then dates and nuts. Stir with fork just until evenly moist.

Spoon into 10 well-greased cups and bake for about 25 minutes. Cool in cups on rack.

Serves 10.

HOLLILEIF B&B
677 Durham Road
Wrightstown/New Hope,
Pennsylvania
18940
(215) 598-3100

MC/V
Moderate

This inn believes in pampering their guests in their romantic, 18th century inn located on 5.5 beautiful country treed acres with gardens and a stream. Comfortable country furnishings and two gas fireplaces help create a pampering atmosphere.

Hollileif B&B
New Hope/Wrightstown, Pennsylvania

SUTTER CREEK INN

Apple Oatmeal Crisp

4 cups tart cooking apples,
   peeled and thinly sliced
1½ tablespoons fresh lemon
   juice
3½ tablespoons granulated
   sugar
⅓ cup all-purpose flour

1 cup rolled oats
½ cup firmly packed brown
   sugar
1 teaspoon cinnamon
1 cup chopped walnuts
½ teaspoon salt
½ cup melted butter

Preheat oven to 375°. Generously butter a 9" square pan.

Combine apples, lemon juice and granulated sugar and put in pan. In a bowl combine flour, oats, brown sugar, cinnamon, walnuts, salt and melted butter and sprinkle over apples. Bake for 35 minutes.

SUTTER CREEK INN
P.O. Box 385
Sutter Creek, California
95685
(209) 267–5606

No credit cards
Expensive

This classic California inn is in a gold rush town popular for antiquing and sightseeing. The inn features swinging beds which can be stabilized, and fireplaces in almost every room.

Sutter Creek Inn
Sutter Creek, California

JOHNSON HOUSE B&B
2278 West 34th Avenue
Vancouver, British
Columbia
Canada
V6M1G6
(604) 266-4175

Moderate

This restored character
home is located in one of
Vancouver's finest neigh-
borhoods. Brass beds, car-
ousel horses, and antique
décor make for a fun and
memorable stay.

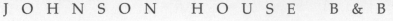

JOHNSON HOUSE B&B

Sandy's Blueberry Muffins

Muffins:
4 cups white flour
3 tablespoons baking powder
½ cup sugar
1 teaspoon salt
3 eggs
2 cups buttermilk
½ cup melted butter

⅔ cup sugar
½ cup oil
2 teaspoons lemon rind
2 cups blueberries

Glaze:
Juice of one lemon (approxi-
    mately ¼ cup)
¾ cup sugar

Preheat oven to 400 degrees.

In a large mixing bowl, mix together flour, baking powder, sugar, and salt. In a separate medium size bowl, mix together the eggs, buttermilk, melted butter, sugar, oil, lemon rind, and blueberries. Add the blueberries mixture to the flour mixture and mix gently, but thoroughly. Scoop batter into greased muffin tins and bake for 20 minutes.

While muffins are baking, prepare the glaze by simply dissolving the sugar in the lemon juice. Once muffins are out of the oven, use approximately one teaspoon of the lemon glaze to cover each muffin. Makes 24 muffins.

Johnson House B&B, Vancouver, BC

S P R I N G   B A N K ,   A   B & B   I N N

Hot Pear Compote

This farm boasts apple, chestnut, walnut and hickory trees. The most bountiful yield, however, comes from 3 aged pear trees whose boughs are heavy with fruit in September and October. These pear recipes are excellent choices for a cool autumn breakfast.

2 cups water	*1 teaspoon cinnamon*
2 tablespoons lemon juice	*8 large pears*
2 tablespoons sugar	*dash of cinnamon*

In a saucepan, bring water, lemon juice, sugar and 1 teaspoon cinnamon to a boil. Peel and halve the pears. Slice into ¼″ pieces. Add pear pieces to boiling syrup. Reduce to medium heat and cook until pears soften (about 10 minutes). Serve immediately, topped with a dash of cinnamon. Serves 4.

Pear Butter

2 cups water	*1 teaspoon cinnamon*
2 tablespoons lemon juice	*8 large pears*
2 tablespoons sugar	

Prepare as for the hot pear compote, but continue to cook until the liquid evaporates and the pears turn to a mash. Refrigerate until ready to use. Spread on toast.

SPRING BANK,
A B&B INN
7945 Worman's Mill Road
Frederick, Maryland
21701
(301) 694–0440

No credit cards
Expensive

Located in historic Frederick, the Spring Bank Farm Inn is set in rolling countryside near parks for hiking and rural roads for exploring and biking.

BRIDGEFORD HOUSE B&B

Denise's Perfect Brownies

2 one ounce squares
    unsweetened chocolate
½ cup butter or margarine
1 cup sugar

2 eggs
1 teaspoon vanilla
½ cup sifted flour
½ cup chopped walnuts

Preheat oven to 325 degrees.

Melt chocolate over hot water. Mix thoroughly butter and sugar. Add eggs and beat well. Blend in melted chocolate, vanilla and flour. Pour into greased 8 by 8 by 2 pan. Sprinkle walnuts evenly over batter.

Bake approximately for 35 minutes. Cool at least one hour before cutting.

BRIDGEFORD HOUSE
B&B
263 Spring Street
Eureka Springs, Arkansas
72632
(501) 253-7853

Moderate
MC/V

An 1884 antique-filled Victorian cottage located on a quiet tree-lined street in the historic district. Close to downtown and shops.

Bridgeford House B&B
Eureka Springs, Arkansas

LITTLE GREENBRIER LODGE

Greenbrier Belgian Waffles

2 cups all-purpose flour, sifted
1 tablespoon baking powder
pinch of salt
1 tablespoon sugar
½ cup half and half

1 stick melted butter
2 eggs, separated
1 teaspoon pure vanilla
non-stick spray

Preheat Belgian waffle iron, or regular waffle iron.

Mix flour, baking powder, salt, sugar, half and half, butter, and egg yolks in a large mixing bowl. In a separate bowl, beat egg whites with vanilla. Fold egg whites and vanilla gradually into mixture.

Spray Belgian waffle iron with non-stick spray. Pour approximately ½ cup of mixture per waffle. Cook as directed by iron, approximately 3–5 minutes. Serve hot and top with one of the following or any combination: whip-cream, powdered sugar, strawberries, and warm pure maple syrup.

Serves 5–6.

LITTLE GREENBRIER
LODGE
3685 Lyon Springs Road
Sevierville, Tennessee
37862
(800) 277-8100
(615) 429-2500

MC/V/DS
Moderate

This rustic lodge is nestled on the mountain surrounded by a beautiful vista, only 150 yards to Great Smoky Mountains. Near Gatlinburg, Dollywood, Pigeon Forge, shopping and hiking.

GOSBY HOUSE INN
Bread Pudding

GOSBY HOUSE INN
643 Light House Avenue
Pacific Grove, California
93950
(408) 375-1287

No credit cards
Very expensive

This elegant 19-room inn is located on the Monterey Peninsula, south of San Francisco, an area of stunning ocean vistas.

6 eggs
2½ cups half-and-half
½ cup sugar
cinnamon, mace and
   nutmeg, to taste

¼ teaspoon salt
8 day-old croissants
¾ cup currants or raisins

Preheat oven to 350°. Butter a 10″ pie plate or quiche dish.

Whisk together eggs, half-and-half, sugar, spices and salt. Pour custard into buttered pan. Break up croissants into bite-sized pieces and spread over custard. Spread currants on top. Press croissants and currants lightly into custard. Bake for about 50 minutes or until it is slightly firm to the touch in the center. Serves 6 to 8.

Gosby House Inn
Pacific Grove, California

THE GOVERNOR'S INN

Iced Christmas Cherry

3 one-pound cans pitted tart
   cherries (packed in
   water)
2 cinnamon sticks
6 whole cloves
6 whole allspice
1 cup water
½ lemon
½ cup sugar
pinch of salt
1 pint heavy cream
1 tablespoon all-purpose
   flour
2 cups French Medoc wine
sweetened whipped cream for
   garnish

Empty two cans tart cherries and juice into a large pot. Add juice from third can, but reserve cherries. Mix in spices, water, lemon, sugar and pinch of salt. Bring to a boil. In a separate smaller pan, scald cream and whisk in flour. Cool scalded mixture slightly and add to berry mixture. Add wine and bring just to the boiling point. Strain out solids and cool mixture. Add the reserved can of berries and refrigerate. This will keep in the refrigerator for at least 2 weeks.

When ready to serve, place about 5 ounces of chilled potable in a glass bowl or compote—a liner bowl set in crushed ice works well for serving—and garnish with a dollop of whipped cream. Serves 12.

THE GOVERNOR'S INN
86 Main Street
Ludlow, Vermont
05149
(802) 228–8830

MC / V / AE
Expensive

This southern Vermont small-town B & B is close to 5 lakes, the Black River and Okemo Mountain. Guests sleep soundly in century-old 4-poster brass beds and delight in 4-course gourmet breakfasts.

STONE HEDGE INN

Southern Pecan Pie

two 10" pastry-lined
   pie shells
7 eggs
1 quart Karo dark corn syrup
1 cup dark brown sugar
4 ounces (1 stick) butter
1 teaspoon salt
3 cups pecans

Preheat oven to 400°.

Pre-bake pastry shells for 10 minutes. Mix together all ingredients except pecans. Fill each shell with 1½ cups of pecans. Pour filling over pecans and bake 40 minutes or until done. Makes 2 pies, each of which serves 6 to 8.

STONE HEDGE INN
Box 366
Tryon, North Carolina
28782
(704) 859–9114

MC / V
Moderate to expensive

Poised in a beautiful mountain setting on the North-South Carolina border, Stone Hedge Inn has 4 rooms and a swimming pool, and serves memorable meals.

ANNIE'S BED & BREAKFAST

Italian Coconut Cream Cake

1 cup (2 sticks) softened
  butter
2 cups sugar
5 egg yolks
2 cups all-purpose flour
1 teaspoon baking soda
1 cup buttermilk
1 teaspoon vanilla
one 3½-ounce can coconut

1 cup nuts
5 egg whites, stiffly beaten
5 tablespoons flour
1 cup milk
1 cup sugar
1 cup softened butter
1 teaspoon vanilla
¼ cup coconut

Preheat oven to 350°. Butter and flour 2 cake pans.

Cream butter and sugar. Beat in egg yolks one at a time. Blend in flour combined with baking soda, alternating with buttermilk. Add vanilla. Beat just until smooth. Stir in coconut and nuts. Gently fold in egg whites. Bake for one hour.

To make the frosting, cook 5 tablespoons flour and 1 cup milk on low heat until thick, stirring constantly. Cool. Cream butter, sugar and vanilla. Beat flour mixture into creamed butter mixture until it is creamy and of a spreading consistency.

Frost cake and sprinkle top and sides of cake with coconut. Serves 12 to 14.

ANNIE'S BED &
BREAKFAST
P.O. Box 928
Big Sandy, Texas
75755
(903) 636-4355
MC / V
Expensive to very
expensive

Annie's Bed & Breakfast is a
unique east Texas Victorian
inn with 13 individually-
decorated rooms and is
home to Annie's Attic, a
national mail-order needle-
craft company.

ALLEN HOUSE VICTORIAN INN

Quick and Easy Banana Blueberry Crumb Cake

1 package Pillsbury banana
   cake mix
2 ripe bananas
1 quart fresh or frozen
   blueberries

1 cup brown sugar
1 tablespoon flour
½ cup chopped walnuts

Preheat oven to 350 degrees.

Follow directions on package of cake mix. Add blueberries and two mashed bananas. Spread mixture in greased 9 by 13 inch baking dish. Mix brown sugar, nuts and flour in separate mixing bowl. Spread topping mixture over the cake.

Bake 30–40 minutes. Let cool slightly before serving.

ALLEN HOUSE
VICTORIAN INN
599 Main Street
Amherst, Massachusetts
01002
(413) 253-5000

Moderate

An authentic antique-filled 1886 Victorian inn on three acres. Spacious bed chambers, private baths, and ceiling fans are the perfect combination for a comfortable stay. Historic Preservation Award winner. Located opposite Emily Dickinson Homestead.

A C W O R T H   I N N

Zesty Cranberry Nut Sweet Rolls

ACWORTH INN
4352 Old Kings Highway
Cummaquid, Massachu-
setts
02637
(800) 362-6363
(508) 362-3330

MC/V/AE
Moderate

This comfortable inn, noted
for its hand painted furnishings, offers Cape Cod charm
in the center of the historic
district. Easy access to
islands as well.

¼ cup orange juice
⅓ cup sweetened dried
   cranberries
¼ cup butter
1 cup buttermilk
2 eggs
¼ cup sugar
1 teaspoon salt
1 tablespoon active dry yeast

4 cups bread flour
⅓ cup coarsely chopped
   roasted pecans or
   walnuts
6 tablespoons butter
   (softened)
zest of one orange finely diced
½ cup sugar
½ cup heavy cream

Preheat oven to 375 degrees.

Rolls: Bring orange juice to boil and pour over cranberries. Let stand for ten minutes. Strain and save liquid. Heat butter with buttermilk until warm (not more than 115 degrees). Place in mixing bowl; add eggs, sugar, salt, and yeast. Mix together. Add flour and knead until smooth and elastic. Add nuts and cranberries; and distribute evenly throughout the dough. Shape into a ball and place in a greased bowl. Turn dough over to coat. Cover with damp cloth and let rise until double—about one hour. Divide in half.

Roll one half into a 12 by 8-inch rectangle. Smooth three tablespoons softened butter on dough. Sprinkle with one-half of the orange zest and ¼ cup sugar. Roll up from long side. Seal seam. Cut twelve even slices. Place rolls cut side down into greased 9 by 1½ inch round baking pan. Repeat with remaining dough. Cover. Each pan of rolls can be refrigerated at this point for up to four days. Let rise until double—about thirty minutes. For a creamier roll, drizzle ¼ cup heavy cream over each pan of rolls.

Bake for 20 minutes or until golden brown. Cool slightly. Drizzle with icing.

Icing: Combine two cups sifted powdered sugar, ¼ teaspoon orange extract, and enough strained orange juice for drizzling.

Makes 24 rolls.

Part 3

T E A T I M E

Teatime

The venerable British tradition of afternoon tea has begun making its appearance on the American scene. Once the preserve of the upper class, it is now enjoying a popularity as an occasion for intimate discussions, informal get-togethers and even business meetings. Although traditionally held between 3:00 and 5:00 P.M., teatime may begin a bit earlier and even run a bit later. Besides tea, such treats as sandwiches, cakes and pastries, crumpets, scones, shortbreads, petit fours and fruits will tempt those who wish to indulge.

For those inns which have adopted the custom, teatime provides a wonderful opportunity for guests and innkeepers to discuss the day's sightseeing and evening dinner plans. At the Mainstay Inn in Cape May, New Jersey, tea is the time when the guests get to know the innkeeper and one another. Guests gather in the dining room or on the veranda or may choose to take their tea and tidbits outside to sit by the garden fountain. Innkeepers say that many a friendship has been cemented over the rim of a teacup.

Each inn has its own special style of serving tea. Ron Gibson, innkeeper of the Victorian Villa in Union City, Michigan, has researched the custom in antique cookbooks and has become an expert in this afternoon affair. To start with, he offers a choice of 30 different teas, including some which he himself blends. To complement the tea, a vast array of delectables are served: perhaps cheese and crackers, meat or cucumber sandwiches, crumpets, smoked fish, scones, tea breads, pastries and fruit. Ron recommends a change of teas midway through the afternoon: maybe starting with a brisk orange pekoe or English breakfast and then switching to an Earl Grey for the sweets.

HISTORIC 1725 WITMER'S TAVERN

Lafayette's Rice Cake

General Lafayette acquired his taste for this cake while recuperating in Bethlehem, Pennsylvania, at the Sun Inn during the Valley Forge winter encampment. Wherever he travelled and found Mennonite cooks, he requested it. At Historic 1725 Witmer's Tavern, this dessert is now served on special occasions.

1 cup softened butter
2 cups sugar
4 egg yolks
2 cups rice flour
1 cup wheat flour
1 teaspoon baking powder

¼ teaspoon nutmeg
2 tablespoons rum or brandy
1 cup milk
4 egg whites, stiffly beaten
powdered sugar (optional)

Preheat oven to 350°. Butter Turk's-head mold (or loaf tin) and lightly dust with flour.

Cream butter and sugar. Add yolks one at a time, beating until creamy. In another bowl, sift rice and wheat flours together with baking powder and nutmeg. Combine rum or brandy with milk in a cup. Blend flour mixture into creamed butter mixture. Gently beat in milk and liquor combination, stopping when a smooth consistency is reached. Fold in beaten egg whites. Transfer to mold and bake for one hour. Cool 15 minutes before removing from pan. Sprinkle powdered sugar over cooled cake, if desired. Yields one cake, which serves 8 to 10.

HISTORIC 1725 WITMER'S TAVERN
2014 Old Philadelphia Pike
Lancaster, Pennsylvania 17602
(717) 299–5305

No credit cards
Moderate to expensive

In the heart of the Pennsylvania Dutch country, the tavern was the starting point for many westward wagon trains and is listed on the National Register of Historic Places.

THE PRESTON HOUSE

Scottish Currant Shortbread

THE PRESTON HOUSE
106 Faithway Street
Santa Fe, New Mexico
87501
(505) 982-3465

MC/V
Expensive

Listed on the National
Register of Historic Places,
the Preston House, just off
the Old Santa Fe Trail, is a
Queen Anne-style house
filled with antiques, fireplaces, fresh flowers and
fruit.

⅓ cups currants or raisins
5 tablespoons fresh orange
   juice
1½ cups all-purpose flour

2 tablespoons sugar
½ cup (1 stick) chilled
   unsalted butter

Preheat oven to 350°. Lightly butter baking sheet.

Bring currants or raisins and 4 tablespoons orange juice to boil in small saucepan, stirring. Remove from heat and let cool. Combine flour and sugar in large bowl. Cut in butter till mixture resembles coarse meal. Stir in fruit mixture and remaining tablespoon orange juice. Knead just till dough holds together. Roll dough out on prepared baking sheet into 10″ by 12″ rectangle. Trim edges and square off corners. Prick surface all over with fork. Sprinkle with sugar. Cut into 24 squares, leaving in place on baking sheet. Bake till pale golden color, 20 to 22 minutes. Re-cut while warm. Cool on rack, then store in airtight container. Yields 24 pieces.

The Preston House
Santa Fe, New Mexico

ELEGANT VICTORIAN MANSION

Madeleines

1 cup butter, softened
2½ cups powdered sugar, sifted
4 eggs
2 cups all-purpose flour

1 teaspoon vanilla or lemon
extract or orange extract
(may add more or less to
taste)

Preheat oven to 350 degrees. Beat the butter until fluffy, add the sugar gradually. Add eggs, one at a time, beating at higher speed after each addition. Add flour gradually and flavoring.

In a Madeleine pan, place one tablespoon batter in each well greased and floured Madeleine cup. Bake 15–20 minutes. Madeleines should be lightly golden. Time is critical. Remove from oven and remove from pan. Cool on rack. Makes 3½ dozen.

If you only have one pan available, clean, dry and butter and dust with flour before starting second batch. Two pans are recommended since recipe makes about 3½ dozen Madeleines. Sprinkle with powdered sugar before serving. Store left-over in an airtight container at room temperature. Madeleines will keep for four to five days.

BEAL HOUSE INN

Crunchy Ginger Snaps

¾ cup margarine
1 cup sugar
¼ cup molasses
1 unbeaten egg

2 cups flour
2 teaspoons baking soda
2 teaspoons ginger
1 teaspoon cinnamon
1 teaspoon salt

Preheat oven to 350 degrees. Cream together margarine, sugar, molasses, and unbeaten egg. Add remaining dry ingredients to wet mixture. Mix together well. Ginger Snap mixture is best handled when chilled for about thirty minutes.

Form Ginger Snaps in balls using approximately two teaspoons of mixture (the size of a large walnut). Roll balls in granulated sugar. Place 2 inches apart on cookie sheet and bake for 12 minutes.

ELEGANT VICTORIAN MANSION
1406 "C" Street
Eureka, California
95501
(800) 386-1888
(707) 444-3144

MC/V
Moderate

This 1888 National Historic Landmark "House-Museum" is perfect for the discriminating connoisseur who appreciates authentic Victorian décor, who has a passion for quality, service and the extra-ordinary.

BEAL HOUSE INN
2 West Main Street
Littleton, New Hampshire
03561
(603) 444-2661

MC/V/AE
Moderate

The Beal House offers a genteel setting for the perfect blend of relaxation and a taste of the past. The inn is located within walking distance of Littleton, quaint shops and tasteful dining.

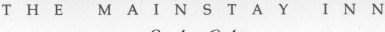

THE MAINSTAY INN

Eccles Cakes

1¾ cup all-purpose flour
2½ teaspoons baking powder
1 tablespoon sugar
¼ teaspoon salt
¼ cup (½ stick) chilled
   butter

2 eggs
⅓ cup light cream
currants or chopped dates
butter and sugar

Preheat oven to 450°. Butter a baking sheet.

Mix flour, baking powder, sugar and salt together. Work butter into flour mixture to form pea-sized pieces. Beat eggs, and reserve two tablespoons of beaten egg. Stir cream into larger quantity of the eggs. Make a large well in the center of flour mixture. Add egg/cream and stir until just blended. Turn out onto a floured board, and knead until the dough loses its stickiness. Roll out to ¾" thickness, and cut into 2½" rounds. Place 1½" apart on the baking sheet. Poke a hole in the center of each round, and fill with currants or chopped dates. Dot each with butter. Fold opposite edges of circle together, and pinch edges closed like a turnover, sealing in filling. Brush tops with reserved egg and sprinkle with sugar. Bake for 12 minutes. Yields one dozen cakes.

THE MAINSTAY INN
635 Columbia Avenue
Cape May, New Jersey
08204
(609) 884-8690

No credit cards
Expensive

The Mainstay Inn was built by two wealthy 19th-century gamblers who spared no expense in its construction.

RED CLOVER INN

Poppy Seed Tea Cake

½ pound softened butter
1 cup sugar
4 egg yolks
¼ cup poppy seeds
2 cups cake flour

1 teaspoon baking soda
½ pint (1 cup) sour cream
4 egg whites, stiffly beaten
1 teaspoon almond extract
1 teaspoon cinnamon

Preheat oven to 350°. Butter a tube pan and lightly dust with flour.

Cream together butter, sugar, egg yolks and poppy seeds. Sift together flour and baking soda. Add flour mixture and sour cream alternately to creamed mixture, beginning and ending with flour mixture. Combine egg whites, almond extract and cinnamon and fold into batter. Pour into tube pan. Bake for one hour or until cake tester comes out clean. Cool on cake rack. Serves 8 to 10.

RED CLOVER INN
Woodward Road
Mendon, Vermont
05701
(802) 775-2290

MC / V / AE / DC
Moderate to expensive

The Red Clover Inn is a country estate hidden in a valley down a country road. The owner, who is also the chef, delights guests with candlelit breakfasts.

*The Red Clover Inn
Mendon, Vermont*

LONGSWAMP BED & BREAKFAST

Carrot-Zucchini Bread

LONGSWAMP B & B
1605 State Street
Mertztown, Pennsylvania
19539
(610) 682-6197

No credit cards
Moderate

This rural inn was once a stop on the underground railroad for slaves escaping the South.

2½ cups unsifted all-purpose
   flour
1 cup unsifted whole wheat
   flour
1 tablespoon baking powder
1 teaspoon baking soda
½ teaspoon salt
½ cup firmly packed brown
   sugar
2 eggs

1½ cups buttermilk
2 tablespoons melted butter
grated rinds of 1 orange and
   1 lemon
1 cup coarsely shredded
   zucchini
1 cup coarsely shredded
   carrots
whipped cream cheese
powdered ginger

Preheat oven to 350°. Butter a 9" by 5" by 3" loaf pan.

Mix together flours, baking powder, soda, salt and sugar. Add remaining ingredients. Stir until well blended. Pour into loaf pan and bake for 1¼ hours or until cake is firm. Cool 5 minutes, then unmold onto a rack. Cool before slicing. When cool, top with whipped cream cheese flavored with a touch of powdered ginger. Yields one loaf, which serves 10.

Longswamp B & B
Mertztown, Pennsylvania

SILVER MAPLE LODGE

Lemon Tea Bread

3 cups flour
1½ teaspoons baking powder
1½ teaspoons baking soda
¼ teaspoon salt
¾ cup butter, softened
1½ cups sugar
3 eggs

pinch of nutmeg
1 tablespoon pure lemon
   extract
1 teaspoon pure vanilla
   extract
1½ cups sour cream

Preheat oven to 315 degrees.

Combine flour, baking soda, baking powder, and salt. Set aside. Beat for two minutes on medium speed butter, sugar, eggs, and extracts. Blend sour cream into egg mixture, then blend flour combination into egg mixture. Pour batter into two greased 8½ by 4½ by 2½ (Baker's Secret) loaf pans. Dust with nutmeg.

Bake for 50–55 minutes (or until the cake tester come out clean).

Serves 8–12.

SILVER MAPLE LODGE
Route 1, Box 8, South Main
Street
Fairlee, Vermont
05045
(800) 666-1946
(802) 333-4326

MC/V
Moderate

This quaint country inn is located in a scenic resort area convenient to antique stores, fishing, golf, swimming, tennis, and winter skiing. Special ballooning packages available.

THE WILDWOOD INN
121 Church Street
Ware, Massachusetts
01082
(413) 967–7798

MC/V/AE
Moderate

The Wildwood Inn is a place to relax and unwind—and maybe take a bicycle ride, a plunge in the swimming hole, a hike or a walk down the local shady lanes. Its unusual collection of American primitive antiques and heirloom quilts make it the perfect backdrop for a visit to nearby Old Sturbridge Village.

W I L D W O O D   I N N
Wildwood's Tea Scones

2 cups sifted all-purpose flour	⅓ cup butter
2 tablespoons sugar	1 egg
3 teaspoons baking powder	½ to ¾ cup milk
½ teaspoon salt	1 egg, lightly beaten (optional)

Preheat oven to 425°. Butter a cookie sheet.

Sift flour, sugar, baking powder and salt together. Work in butter until particles are the size of coarse cornmeal. Combine egg and about ½ cup milk. Stir liquids quickly and lightly into the dry ingredients until dough is moistened. The less milk the better, but add a little more if needed, to make a soft dough.

Grease your hands and turn the dough out onto a floured dish towel. Knead gently 15 times. Cut dough in half. Shape each half into a ball and press down to form a round, approximately ¼" thick. Cut each into 8 wedges, like a pie, using a floured knife. Place wedges on a greased cookie sheet or pie tin, without allowing them to touch. Bake for 10 to 15 minutes. If you'd like them to shine, glaze with lightly-beaten egg before baking. Scones should be golden brown when done. Yields 16 scones, which serve 6 to 8.

T A U G H A N N O C K   F A R M S   I N N
Orange Date Bread

rind of 1 orange	1 cup (2 sticks) butter
1 cup water	2 cups all-purpose flour
½ cup chopped dates	2 teaspoons baking powder
¾ cup sugar	½ teaspoon salt
2 tablespoons butter	
1 egg, beaten	

Preheat oven to 350°. Generously butter an 8" by 4" loaf pan.

TAUGHANNOCK FARMS INN

Mix together the first 3 ingredients in a saucepan and boil gently. Add sugar and butter, stir until dissolved and remove from heat. When cooled, stir in remaining ingredients. Put in a loaf pan and bake for about 45 minutes or until it tests done. Serve sliced, with cream cheese. Yields one loaf, which serves 8 to 10.

MANOR HOUSE
A to Z Bread

3 cups flour	1 cup oil
1 teaspoon salt	2 cups sugar
1 teaspoon baking soda	2 cups A to Z mix (see below)
3 teaspoons cinnamon	3 teaspoons vanilla
½ teaspoon baking powder	1 cup chopped nuts
3 eggs	

Preheat oven to 325 degrees.

A to Z mix: Use one or a combination to equal two cups (except as indicated): grated apples, applesauce, chopped apricots, mashed bananas, grated carrots, pitted and chopped cherries, freshly ground coconut, pitted and chopped dates, ground eggplant, finely chopped figs, seedless grapes, honey (omit sugar), ½ cup lemon juice, marmalade (omit 1 cup sugar), mincemeat, chopped oranges, chopped fresh or canned peaches, ½ cup peppermint, chopped pears, drained crushed pineapple, 1 cup chopped pitted prunes, canned pumpkin, raisins, raspberries, chopped rhubarb, fresh or frozen (drained) strawberries, cooked tapioca, grated sweet potatoes, tomatoes (add an extra ½ cup sugar), cooked and mashed yams, plain or flavored yogurt, and grated zucchini.

Sift dry ingredients and set aside. Beat eggs in a large bowl. Add oil and sugar, cream well. Add A to Z mix and vanilla to mixture. Add sifted dry ingredients. Mix well and stir in chopped nuts. Spoon into two-well greased loaf pans. Bake for 1 hour.

Makes 2 loaves.

TAUGHANNOCK FARMS INN
2030 Gorge Road
Trumansburg, New York 14886
(607) 387-7711

No credit cards
Moderate

The Taughannock Farms Inn is set among some of central New York State's most spectacular scenery: Taughannock Falls and Gorge and Cayuga Lake.

MANOR HOUSE
69 Maple Avenue
Norfolk, Connecticut 06058
(860) 542-5690

Most Credit Cards
Expensive

A historic Victorian mansion furnished with genuine antiques, located on five splendid acres. Romantic, elegantly appointed bedrooms. Breakfast in bed as well as sleigh and carriage rides available. Concert series.

HEADLANDS INN
P.O. Box 132
Mendocino, California
95460
(707) 937-4431

No credit cards
Expensive

A comfortable restored Victorian home nestled in a northern California village, the Headlands has many rooms with ocean views.

H E A D L A N D S   I N N

Headlands Inn Lemon Bread

1 cup softened butter
2 cups sugar
4 eggs
½ teaspoon salt
½ teaspoon soda
3 cups all-purpose flour

1 cup buttermilk
1 cup chopped nuts
grated rind of 1 lemon
juice of 3 lemons
1 cup sugar

Preheat oven to 350°. Butter and flour two 7″ by 3″ by 2″ loaf pans.

Cream butter and 2 cups sugar. Beat in eggs, one at a time. Sift together salt, soda, and flour, and add alternately, with the buttermilk, to the creamed butter and sugar. Begin and end with the dry ingredients. Fold in the nuts and rind. Bake for 40 minutes to one hour or until tests done.

Heat lemon juice and sugar long enough for the sugar to dissolve. Place warm loaves of bread on foil and spoon juice topping over them. Yields 2 loaves, each of which serves 8.

Headlands Inn
Mendocino, California

D A R B Y   F I E L D   I N N

Chocolate Paté
with White Chocolate Sauce

Chocolate Paté:
8 ounces bittersweet chocolate
4 ounces butter
4 whole eggs
1 egg yolk
2 egg whites

Preheat oven to 325 degrees.

Melt chocolate and butter in double boiler. Cool chocolate.

In a separate boiler, warm 4 whole eggs plus 1 egg yolk (do not overheat), whipping constantly once eggs are warm. Beat in mixer until eggs fall off beaters in a ribboning fashion.

Once chocolate has cooled, fold eggs and chocolate together.

Beat two egg whites until stiff peaks form. Fold into chocolate mixture and pour into buttered loaf pan. Bake in a hot-water bath for 45 minutes, or until knife comes out clean.

White Chocolate Sauce:
5 ounches white chocolate,
*   melted*
2½ ounces heavy cream

Combine melted white chocolate with heavy cream (both ingredients should be room temperature when combined).

Serves 8.

Serving Suggestions:
Refrigerate paté overnight. Slice as you would a loaf of bread. Serve warmed slightly with warm white chocolate sauce and an edible flower (i.e.: nasturtium or pansy) for garnish.

DARBY FIELD INN
P.O. Box D, Bald Hill Road
Conway, New Hampshire
03818
(800) 426-4147
(603) 447-2181

MC/V/AE
Moderate

A cozy inn overlooking Mount Washington Valley, Presidential Mountains, and rivers. Fifteen miles of cross-country skiing, outdoor pool, and candlelight dinners await.

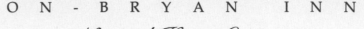

VON-BRYAN INN
Nut and Honey Crisp

VON-BRYAN INN
2402 Hatcher Mountain
Road
Sevierville, Tennessee
(423) 453-9832

V/MC/AE
Moderate

When staying at the Von-
Bryan Inn, one may enjoy
the majestic views of the
Great Smoky Mountains.
The old-fashioned hospitality is enticing and the
atmosphere is relaxed. Take
time off and enjoy this mar-
velous Inn.

4 cups peeled, sliced apples
¼ cup sugar
1 tablespoon lemon juice
½ cup honey
1 cup all-purpose flour

½ cup packed brown sugar
½ teaspoon salt
½ cup butter or margarine
½ cup chopped nuts

Preheat oven to 375°. Spread apples in a 1½ quart baking dish. Sprinkle with granulated sugar and lemon juice. Pour honey over all.

Mix flour, brown sugar and salt in bowl and work in butter, making a crumbly mixture. Add nuts. Spread over apples and bake for 40 minutes or until apples are tender and crust is crisp and brown.

THE BRITT HOUSE
White Bread

Great for tea sandwiches.

¼ cup butter, melted and
   cooled slightly
1 tablespoon sugar
2 tablespoons yeast

2 teaspoons salt (optional)
2 cups water, lukewarm
up to 6 cups all-purpose
   flour

Combine first 5 ingredients and mix well. Gradually add up to 6 cups flour, a cup at a time, until the dough forms a ball and leaves the sides of the bowl. Turn onto floured surface and knead until dough becomes elastic to the touch, yet is soft as a baby's cheek. Turn into a greased bowl and let rise in warm spot until doubled in bulk. Shape into 2 standard loaves in loaf pans, or divide into eight 3" by 5" pans. Let rise again until double. Bake at 350° for 20 minutes or until golden and hollow at the top. Yields 2 loaves, approximately 20 slices each.

WHITEGATE INN

Traditional Raisin Scones

3 cups white flour
1 tablespoon baking powder
½ pound unsalted butter –
    soft
¼ cup and 2 tablespoons
    sugar

3 large eggs
⅓ cup buttermilk
½ cup golden raisins

Preheat oven to 350 degrees.

Mix flour and baking powder in bowl. Beat butter until creamy in separate bowl. Add sugar to creamed butter, beating until pale and fluffy. Add eggs one at a time. Add flour mixture and buttermilk. Sprinkle raisins over batter and slowly fold into mixture. Using an ice cream scoop, place mounds of dough on cookie sheet. Bake for 30 minutes.

Makes 1 dozen.

WHITEGATE INN
P.O. Box 150
Mendocino, California
95640
(800) 531-7282
(707) 937-4892

MC/V/AE
Moderate

Located in historic Mendocino, all rooms have been redecorated with French or Victorian antiques. Gourmet breakfasts served in dining room. Ocean views and gardens create the perfect getaway atmosphere.

Whitegate Inn
Mendocino, California

PUDDING CREEK INN
Sugar Crisp Twisties

1 package active dry yeast
¼ cup lukewarm water
3½ cups sifted all-purpose
   flour
1½ teaspoon salt

1 cup (2 sticks) chilled butter
2 eggs, lightly beaten
½ cup sour cream
3 teaspoons vanilla
1½ cup sugar

Preheat oven to 375°.

Proof yeast in warm water. Sift flour and salt into mixing bowl. Cut in butter until particles are fine. Blend in eggs, sour cream, 1 teaspoon vanilla and yeast. Mix well. Cover and chill at least 2 hours. (Dough may be stored in refrigerator for up to 4 days, shaped and baked as needed.) Combine sugar and 2 teaspoons vanilla. Sprinkle ½ cup on rolling surface. Roll out half the dough on vanilla-sugar mixture to a 16″ by 8″ shape. Sprinkle with about one tablespoon of the vanilla-sugar. Fold one end of the dough over the center, then fold other end to make 3 layers. Turn dough ¼ of the way around, repeat rolling, folding and sprinkling. Roll out to 16″ by 8″. Cut into strips. Twist each strip 2 or 3 times. Place on un-greased cookie sheets. Repeat process with remaining dough and vanilla-sugar mixture. Bake for 15 to 20 minutes until golden brown. Serves 8 to 10.

PUDDING CREEK INN

Cheese Fingers

16 ounces softened cream
    cheese
½ cup sugar
4 egg yolks
1 teaspoon vanilla or almond
    extract

1 box phyllo dough
½ pound (2 sticks) butter,
    melted
chopped almonds (optional)

Preheat oven to 375°.

Blend together cream cheese, sugar, egg yolks and vanilla or almond extract to make the filling. Unwrap phyllo dough and cover with damp towel, so that the dough doesn't dry out. Lay out one sheet of dough and brush with melted butter. Fold over the top half of the sheet. Brush again with butter. Put 2 teaspoons of filling at one long end. Take wide ends and fold ½" in on each side. Starting at filling end, roll up into a "finger." Brush with butter. Put seam-side down on ungreased cookie sheet. Sprinkle with almonds, if desired. Repeat with remaining dough and filling. Bake for 10 to 15 minutes, or until brown. Serves 6 to 8.

PUDDING CREEK INN
700 North Main Street
Fort Bragg, California
95437
(707) 964-9529

MC/V
Moderate

At the Pudding Creek Inn, built in 1884 by a Russian count, breakfast is served in an enclosed flower-filled fountain courtyard.

Pudding Creek Inn
Fort Bragg, California

TORCH AND TOES B&B
309 South 3rd Avenue
Bozeman, Montana
59715
(406) 586-7285

MC/V
Moderate

A friendly cat, a unique collection of dolls, brass rubbings, and a gourmet breakfast make for a pleasant stay in this central location. Nearby skating, market, and band concerts makes this B&B close to all the fun.

LAMOTHE HOUSE
621 Esplanade Avenue
New Orleans, Louisiana
70116
(504) 947-1161

MC/V/AE
Very expensive

One of New Orleans's classic bed and breakfast inns, the Lamothe House captures all the charm of the city's French Quarter.

TORCH AND TOES B & B
Overnight Coffee Cake

2 cups flour
½ teaspoon salt
1 teaspoon baking soda
1 teaspoon baking powder
¾ cup butter
½ cup sugar
½ cup brown sugar
2 eggs, beaten

1 cup buttermilk
1 teaspoon vanilla

Topping:
½ cup brown sugar
1 teaspoon cinnamon
½ cup chopped nuts

Preheat oven to 350 degrees. Sift together dry ingredients. Cream together butter and both sugars. Add beaten eggs. Add flour alternately with buttermilk. Add vanilla. Pour into greased 9 by 13 inch pan. Sprinkle on topping.

Bake for 35 minutes or cover with aluminum foil and place in refrigerator overnight to bake in morning. Serves 8–10.

LAMOTHE HOUSE
Lamothe House Pecan Pralines

1½ cups granulated sugar
½ cup brown sugar
½ cup evaporated milk
½ stick (4 tablespoons) butter

1 teaspoon vanilla
½ cup chopped or whole
    pecans
1 pinch baking soda

Butter cookie sheet or line with waxed paper.

Cook sugars and milk over medium heat, stirring until mixture starts to boil. Add butter, pecans and soda. Cook, stirring occasionally until it reaches the soft ball stage (when a bit of the candy dropped in cold water forms a soft ball) or 238° on a candy thermometer. Remove from fire, add vanilla and beat with spoon until mixture is creamy and begins to thicken. Drop by teaspoonfuls onto cookie sheet. (If mixture becomes too hard, return to heat and add a little water.)

Makes 12 large or 24 small pralines.

CLEFTSTONE MANOR

Petticoat Tails

1½ cups (3 sticks) butter
1 cup granulated sugar
2 teaspoons vanilla
1½ tablespoons milk

3¾ cups unsifted all-purpose
    flour
3 tablespoons powdered
    sugar (optional)

Preheat oven to 325°.

With electric mixer, beat butter, sugar and vanilla until light and fluffy. Stir in milk and flour using a wooden spoon, then mix with hand until dough is smooth. Divide dough into 3 parts. On ungreased cookie sheets, roll out dough, one part at a time, into ¼" thick 9" rounds. Place 7" plate in centers of rounds, and cut around plate with a fluted pastry cutter. Remove plate. Cut into 8 sections. Bake 25 minutes. Cool completely. Sprinkle with confectioner's sugar if desired.

CLEFTSTONE MANOR
92 Eden Street
Bar Harbor, Maine
04609
(207) 288-4951

MC/V/AE
Moderate to expensive

Located on a windswept cliff at the foot of Cadillac Mountain, the century-old Cleftstone Manor offers a relaxing refuge from everyday life.

Cleftstone Manor
Bar Harbor, Maine

HARBIN HOT SPRINGS
P.O. Box 782
Middletown, California
95461
(707) 987-2477

No credit cards
Inexpensive to moderate

This 1,100-acre bathing-suit-optional hot springs resort is set in the hills just above northern California's Napa Valley.

THE SHELBURNE INN
Pacific Highway 103 and
J Street
P.O. Box 250
Seaview, Washington
98644
(206) 642-2442

MC/V
Expensive

Located on the Pacific coast in the southwest corner of Washington state, the Shelburne Inn has 14 rooms and a restaurant that serves nationally-acclaimed cuisine.

HARBIN HOT SPRINGS

Anna's Lemonade

2½ cups honey (star thistle
   or other light honey)
2½ cups water
2 cups fresh lemon juice, or to
   taste

water
3 tablespoons spearmint
   leaves

Blend honey, 2½ cups water and lemon juice in a blender. Pit in a gallon container. Fill to ¾ of a gallon with additional water. Add spearmint leaves and allow to steep. Serve over ice. Yields 16 cups.

SHELBURNE INN

Lemon Curd

Originally created as a tea-time condiment for scones and crumpets, lemon curd is also delicious on muffins, toast, waffles or pancakes.

1 cup fresh-squeezed lemon
   juice
7 tablespoons lemon zest (the
   outermost part of lemon
   rind)

1 pound (about 2 cups) sugar
¼ pound (1 stick) butter
8 eggs, lightly beaten

Combine lemon juice, zest, sugar and butter in a double-boiler over simmering water until sugar dissolves and butter melts. Whisk eggs into lemon mixture and keep stirring until thick (about 20 minutes). Remove from heat, cool and store in refrigerator. Yields about 5 cups.

G R A F T O N I N N

Orange-Nut Bread

1 medium sized orange	2 cups flour
boiling water	¼ teaspoon salt
1 cup raisins or dates	1 teaspoon baking powder
2 tablespoons shortening	½ teaspoon baking soda
1 teaspoon vanilla	1 cup sugar
1 beaten egg	½ cup chopped nuts

Preheat oven to 350 degrees.

Place juice from orange in a measuring cup and fill with boiling water. Force orange rind and raisins or pitted dates through coarse blade of the food processor. Add diluted orange juice. Stir in shortening, vanilla and egg. Add flour sifted with salt, baking powder, baking soda, and sugar. Beat well and stir in nuts.

Bake in greased one-pound loaf pan for approximately 1 hour.

Serves 8–12.

*Grafton Inn
Falmouth, Cape Cod
Massachusetts*

GRAFTON INN
261 Grand Avenue South
Falmouth, Cape Cod, Massachusetts
02540
(800) 642-4069
(508) 540-8688

MC/V
Moderate

A beautiful oceanfront property with panoramic views. Scrumptious breakfasts including delectable croissants from France. Beach chairs and towels provide a comfortable, relaxed atmosphere on the beach. The inn is conveniently located close to the ferry, shops, and restaurants.

INNSBRUCK INN
233 West Main Street
Aspen, Colorado
81611
(970) 925-2980

MC/V/AE/CB/DC
Expensive to very
expensive

At the family-operated Innsbruck Inn, guests will enjoy a breakfast buffet before a busy day on the slopes, and a sauna and glass of wine après ski. Many friendships are formed here, and groups return together year after year.

INNSBRUCK INN

Champagne Punch

2 cups sugar
4 cups water
½ cup lemon juice
½ cup lime juice

4½ cups orange juice
2 cups grapefruit juice
2 cups Rhine wine
1 bottle champagne

In a saucepan, combine sugar with 2 cups water and lemon juice and boil one minute. Add remaining water and let cool. Stir in lime, orange and grapefruit juices. Pour into bowl filled with ice. Add wine and champagne just before serving. Yields approximately 30 servings.

GUSTAVUS INN

Spruce Tip Beer

green tips of spruce branches
   (gathered in early
   spring)*

boiling water
sugar
yeast

In early spring, gather a peck of new bright green tips of the spruce branches. Cover with boiling water, and let the mixture cool. Drain the liquid from the spruce tips and to 2½ gallons of the liquid add 2 pounds of sugar and ⅛ teaspoon of yeast dissolved in 2 tablespoons of water. Stir all together until sugar and yeast are completely dissolved. Bottle immediately and store in a warm place for 4 or 5 days before opening. Chill bottles before opening. Each gallon fills about ten 12-ounce bottles. This is a cooling non-alcoholic drink.

*If spruce tips are gathered when no longer tiny and new, the beer will take on a strong flavor and will be so effervescent that the bottles may burst.

G U S T A V U S   I N N

Raspberry Shrub

cider vinegar   *sugar*
raspberries   *soda water or cold water*

Pour enough cider vinegar over raspberries to cover the berries. Let this stand, covered with a clean cloth, for 24 hours to 2 days. Strain through a couple thicknesses of cheese-cloth, squeezing the berries to extract all the juice. To every pint of liquid, add a scant cup of sugar. Bring to a boil, and boil gently for 20 minutes. Let cool slightly, and pour into glass jars or bottles. Keep in a cool, dark place until needed. Serve as a beverage, pouring 2 tablespoons of the shrub over ice cubes and filling the glass to the top with cold water or soda water. Each cup of shrub makes 8 drinks.

GUSTAVUS INN
Box 60
Gustavus, Alaska
99826
(907) 697-2254

No credit cards
Expensive

This 7-room summertime Glacier Bay inn offers delightful local dishes, with fresh fish and eggs, vegetables picked from the garden, and berries for jam plucked from bushes in nearby fields and forests.

Gustavus Inn
Gustavus, Alaska

JOHN RUTLEDGE HOUSE
Biscuits with Hot Sherried Fruit

JOHN RUTLEDGE HOUSE
116 Broad Street
Charleston, South Carolina
29401
(800) 476-9741
(803) 723-7999

MC/V/AE
Expensive

John Rutledge, a signer of
the U.S. Constitution, built
this elegant home in 1763.
Visit and relive history. The
inn is located downtown
near shopping and historic
sites.

Fruit:
3 5½-ounce cans pineapple
   chunks in syrup
1 16-ounce can sliced peaches
   in syrup
1 16-ounce can halved pears
   in syrup
½ cup (packed) golden brown
   sugar
6 tablespoons cream Sherry
1 tablespoon fresh lemon juice
1¼ teaspoons ground
   cinnamon
1 tablespoon cornstarch

Biscuits:
2 cups self-rising flour
¼ teaspoon baking soda
⅓ cup frozen solid vegetable
   shortening, cut into pieces
1 cup buttermilk, chilled

Preheat oven to 450 degrees.

Fruit: Drain all fruit, reserving ¼ cup peach syrup. Place fruit in medium saucepan. Stir in sugar, Sherry, lemon juice, and cinnamon; let stand until sugar dissolves. Mix cornstarch and ¼ cup peach syrup in small bowl. Stir into fruit. Cook over high heat until syrup boils and thickens, stirring occasionally, about 3 minutes. (Can be made one day ahead. Chill.)

Biscuits: Dust baking sheet with flour. Sift flour and baking soda together into large bowl. Rub in shortening with fingertips until mixture resembles coarse meal. Gradually add buttermilk, tossing until moist clumps form. Gather dough into ball. Gently knead dough on floured work surface until dough just holds together. Pat out dough to ¾-inch thickness. Using 3-inch round cookie cutter cut out biscuits. Gather scraps; pat out to ¾-inch thickness and cut enough biscuits to equal six in total. Transfer to prepared baking sheet. Bake until light brown, about 15 minutes.

Meanwhile, re-warm fruit mixture over low heat. Serve biscuits with fruit.

Serves 6.

BRIAR ROSE B & B

Strawberry Preserves

4 cups strawberries, cleaned   3 cups sugar
   and hulled

To make more or less preserves, use ¾ cup sugar for every cup of strawberries. Place strawberries in a bowl, layering with sugar. Allow to stand for 12 hours. In a saucepan, bring quickly to boiling point and simmer for 15 minutes. Place in a crock or enamel bowl, cover and allow to steep for another 12 hours. Return to pot just to reheat, then put the preserves in sterilized jars. Seal with paraffin. Yields 2 pints.

Orange Marmalade

2 large oranges   11 cups water
2 large lemons   8 cups sugar

Cut fruit into quarters and remove seeds. Soak the fruit in the water for 24 hours. Drain, reserving the liquid. Cut pulp into shreds. Return to the soaking water and boil for one hour. Add the sugar. Boil until juice forms a jelly. Cool, and put in hot sterilized jars. Seal with paraffin. (Add more lemons if a tarter marmalade is preferred. Emily Hunter at Briar Rose makes her marmalade on the tart side and uses coarsely cut rind.) Yields 2 quarts.

BRIAR ROSE
BED & BREAKFAST
2151 Arapahoe Avenue
Boulder, Colorado
80302

(303) 442-3007
MC / V / AE
Moderate to expensive

Guests at this English country-style home find chocolates on their pillows at bedtime and a decanter of sherry always proffered in the dining room.

THE WEDGWOOD INN
111 West Bridge Street
New Hope, Pennsylvania
18938
(215) 862–2570

No credit cards
Moderate to expensive

The innkeepers of this Victorian mansion in New Hope promise to make their guests' stays as pleasant as the surroundings.

THE WEDGWOOD INN
Hot Buttered Wedgwood

Carl Glassman makes his own liqueur, which he calls Wedgwood Almond Liqueur, to use in this recipe. A carafe of the liqueur is served to guests at their bedside as part of the evening ritual.

2 ounces almond liqueur
1 cup hot tea, cider or apple
  juice
1 tablespoon whipped
  unsalted butter

twist of orange peel
cinnamon stick

Pour almond liqueur in a mug. Fill with hot tea, cider or juice. Add butter and orange peel twist. Garnish with a cinnamon stick.

The Wedgwood Inn
New Hope, Pennsylvania

ROSE MANOR B & B

Brie & Apple Salad Tea Sandwiches

1 cup diced, ripe Brie
1 cup diced, peeled apple
¼ cup chopped walnuts
2 tablespoons sour cream
2 tablespoons mayonnaise
whole wheat or pumpernickel
    bread

Combine Brie, apple and nuts. Blend mayonnaise with sour cream. Add to Brie mixture. Serve on thin slices of whole wheat or pumpernickel bread, crusts removed.

Serves 4.

Rose Manor B&B
Manheim, Pennsylvania

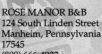

ROSE MANOR B&B
124 South Linden Street
Manheim, Pennsylvania
17545
(800) 666-4932
(717) 664-4932

MC/V
Moderate

A Lancaster Country 1905 manor house. Comfortable décor and cooking reflect "herbal" theme. Near antiques, Pennsylvania Dutch attractions, and Hershey.

BISHOPSGATE INN
Goodspeed Landing
P.O. Box 290, East Haddam,
Connecticut
06423
(860) 873-1677

No credit cards
Moderate

Within walking distance of the famous Goodspeed Opera House, this 1818 colonial home is also near many sites of historical interest.

**LUMBERMAN'S
MANSION INN**
P.O. Box 885
Hayward, Wisconsin
54843
(715) 634-3012

MC/V
Moderate

An elegant 1887 Victorian with antique furnishings, modern luxuries, and immaculate rooms. Gourmet breakfasts prepared featuring regional delicacies. Hospitality and privacy abound.

BISHOPSGATE INN

Minted Raspberry Cooler Bishopsgate Inn

½ cup fresh mint leaves
   plus mint sprigs for
   garnish
1 cup boiling water
one 6-ounce can frozen
   lemonade concentrate

1 pint fresh raspberries
   crushed and sweetened
   with ½ cup sugar (or one
   10-ounce package frozen
   raspberries)
crushed ice
2 cups cold water

Combine ½ cup mint leaves and boiling water. Let steep 5 minutes. Add raspberries and frozen lemonade concentrate. Stir (until thawed, if frozen raspberries are used). Strain into pitcher half-filled with crushed ice. Add cold water and stir. Garnish with fresh mint leaves. Serves 8.

LUMBERMAN'S MANSION INN

Great Grandma's Drop Doughnuts

1 egg, slightly beaten
½ cup sugar
2 tablespoons oil
½ cup milk

1½ cups flour
1 tablespoon baking powder
1 teaspoon nutmeg

Beat egg slightly. Add sugar, oil, and milk. Sift dry ingredients and add to egg mixture, stirring well. Dough will be slightly stiff. Refrigerate dough while heating the oil for frying.

Heat oil to 350 degrees and drop dough by the teaspoon. Turn once. Fry until brown and cooked all the way through. Drain. Shake in a bag of powdered sugar or a combination of cinnamon and sugar. Enjoy warm.

Wonderful with tea, coffee, or hot chocolate on a cold afternoon.

Part 4

HORS D'OEUVRES

Hors d'Oeuvres

Many of the recipes in the preceding chapter on tea are also suitable for hors d'oeuvres. Indeed, many inns offer sherry or other wines right along with tea, forming a consolidated teatime–cocktail hour. Inns that follow the custom of wine and hors d'oeuvres usually do so between 6:00 and 8:00 P.M., when guests have had a chance to relax in their rooms and change into evening clothes, then congregate for a little conviviality before a night on the town.

Innkeepers at the Wedgwood in New Hope, Pennsylvania, serve a house liqueur in their blue-and-cream-colored parlor. While sipping a Wedgwood liqueur, one can sit in the bay window and chat with a friend or play Scrabble® or Trivial Pursuit®.

San Francisco's Petite Auberge offers hors d'oeuvres around the fireplace in the lower parlor. Guests gather to discuss their day in the city and make plans for dinner that evening.

The hors d'oeuvres dishes in this book will be interesting additions to your next party tray. With such selections as Tom's Treat, *Huîtres des Gourmets* and Goat Cheese Turnovers, you'll be able to introduce your guests to some exciting new treats.

SOCIETY HILL HOTEL

Arlene's Artichokes

cooking oil for deep frying
30 artichoke hearts,
    parboiled; or 3 cans of
    artichokes packed in
    water (approximately 10
    per can), drained
6 eggs, lightly beaten

2 cups Italian bread crumbs
1½ cups (3 sticks) butter
juice of 1½ lemons
3 cloves garlic, minced
3 teaspoons minced chives
Parmesan cheese to taste

Cut artichokes in half. Dip in beaten egg and coat with bread crumbs. Deep-fry until golden brown. Put on serving plate and keep warm. Melt butter, add lemon juice, garlic and chives.

Pour butter sauce over artichoke hearts and sprinkle with Parmesan cheese. Serves 6.

SOCIETY HILL HOTEL
OF PHILADELPHIA
301 Chestnut Street
Philadelphia,
Pennsylvania 19106
(215) 925–1919

MC / V / AE
Expensive

Located in Philadelphia's Historic Park, the Society Hill Hotel offers entertainment at its piano bar and fresh flowers and chocolates in each of its 12 rooms.

Society Hill Hotel
Philadelphia, Pennsylvania

GARLAND'S OAK CREEK LODGE

Wild Mushroom Paté

½ pound (2 sticks) unsalted
   butter
½ yellow onion, chopped
2 cloves garlic, minced
1½ pounds fresh boletus
   mushrooms, gently
   rinsed and chopped

1 tablespoon fresh parsley
1 tablespoon fresh thyme
½ cup dry white wine
⅛ cup dry sherry
salt and pepper to taste

Melt butter, add onion and garlic, and cook gently for a
minute. Add boletus, parsley and thyme, and cook over
moderate heat until mushrooms give off their juices. Stir in
wine and sherry. Cook, stirring occasionally, until liquid is
reduced and thickened slightly. Cool briefly, then purée in
food processor until smooth. Season to taste with salt and
pepper. Pour into individual ramekins and chill until set.
Serve with minced red onion and toast. Serves 4 to 6.

GARLAND'S OAK
CREEK LODGE
P.O. Box 152
Sedona, Arizona
86339
(520) 282-3343

MC/V
Expensive

Garland's Oak Creek Lodge
consists of rustic log cabins
scattered across lawns
amidst apple and peach orchards, with Oak Creek
running alongside.

Garland's Oak Creek Lodge
Sedona, Arizona

T R O U T B E C K

Goat Cheese and Seafood Turnovers

DOUGH:
¼ cup heavy cream
¼ cup sour cream
1 egg

2 cups all-purpose flour
salt and pepper to taste

Combine heavy cream, sour cream and egg, then mix in flour, salt and pepper. Knead dough on floured surface until smooth. Let rest one hour in refrigerator, then roll out ⅛" thick. Cut circles with a 2" cookie cutter. While dough is chilling, prepare:

CHEESE FILLING:
½ pound chèvre
¼ pound muenster
⅛ teaspoon pepper

pinch of salt
pinch of nutmeg

Crumble cheese together. Mix in spices and set aside.

SEAFOOD STUFFING:
1 large onion, minced
1 small green pepper, diced
⅓ pound scallops, chopped
⅓ pound shrimp, peeled, deveined and chopped

⅓ pound clams, chopped
salt and pepper to taste
pinch each of oregano, cumin
    and flour
2 tablespoons water

Sauté onion until transparent. Add pepper, seafood, seasonings and water. Cook for 2 minutes while stirring. Set aside and let cool.

ASSEMBLY:

Brush edges of dough circles with water. Place ½ teaspoon of filling in middle. Fold dough over filling, like a turnover. Using the tines of a fork, press along edge of turnover, sealing well. Heat oil for frying. Place turnovers in oil and fry on each side until golden brown. Yields approximately 6 dozen turnovers.

TROUTBECK
Leedsville Road
Amenia, New York
12501
(914) 373–9681

AE
Very expensive

This posh 422-acre country estate operates as an inn on the weekends and a conference center during the week and has been praised by *New York Magazine*, *The New York Times*, *Good Housekeeping* and *Country Living*.

TRILLIUM HOUSE
P.O. Box 280 / Nellysford
Wintergreen, Virginia
22958
(800) 325-9126
(804) 325-9126

MC/V
Moderate

One of the newer country inns, built in 1983 to meet today's standards while keeping yesterday's charm. Located in the beautiful mountain country where trees and birds can be seen from the breakfast table.

TRILLIUM HOUSE

Virginia Ham Tarts

4 sheets Phyllo dough
4 tablespoons butter, melted
non-stick spray
1 cup finely chopped Virginia
    ham (cooked)
1 cup sharp cheddar cheese

¾ cup shredded tart apple
¼ cup ground Ritz cracker
    crumbs
4 miniature muffin tins
    (12 compartments each)

Preheat oven to 350 degrees.

Lay one sheet of Phyllo on a large cutting board and brush with some of the melted butter. Repeat with second and third sheets, stacking on top of the previous as you go, and ending with fourth sheet unbuttered. Cut rectangular stack into 48 squares (6 length-wise cuts, 8 short-wise cuts) and press into muffin tins that have been coated with non-stick spray.

Combine ham, cheese, apple and cracker crumbs in a bowl and press about one tablespoon into each Phyllo shell (may be done several hours ahead to this point, wrap and refrigerate).

Bake for 15 to 20 minutes, until golden brown.

Makes 48 miniature tarts.

THISTLE AND SHAMROCK INN

Chicken Liver Paté

¾ pound diced bacon
2 large onions, diced
4 cloves of garlic, chopped
4 bay leaves
4 whole cloves
scant teaspoon whole thyme
½ teaspoon whole oregano
1 pound plus 12 ounces fresh
   chicken livers

7 whole eggs, whipped
12 ounces butter, softened
1 teaspoon Maggi seasoning
4 teaspoons Worcestershire
   sauce
½ teaspoon Tabasco sauce
salt and pepper to taste

Preheat oven to 500 degrees. In an oven-proof pot, combine bacon, onions, garlic, and spices and cook thoroughly on the stovetop. Add chicken livers and cook until well done. Place pot in preheated oven for 10 minutes, stirring occasionally. Whip eggs and stir into chicken liver mixture—leave in oven 10 more minutes. Remove from oven, cool, and process until smooth in a food processor. Chill thoroughly.

When cold, place the liver mixture in a mixing bowl and whip on medium speed for 10 minutes. Add the softened butter and whip an additional 10 minutes. Season with Maggi, Worcestershire sauce, Tabasco sauce, salt and pepper. Chill before serving. May be served with your favorite cracker or bread toasts.

THISTLE AND
SHAMROCK INN
11 West Main Street
Bradford, New Hampshire
03221
(888) 938-5553
(603) 938-5553

All major credit cards
Moderate

A wonderful old hotel, built at the turn of the century, where you can relax and enjoy a comfortable environment.

Thistle & Shamrock Inn,
Bradford, New Hampshire

GRÜNBERG HAUS
R.R. 2, Box 1595
Waterbury, Vermont
05676
(802) 244-7726
(800) 800-7760

MC/V/AE
Moderate

Spontaneous, personal attention in a hand-built Austrian chalet.

G R Ü N B E R G   H A U S

Hot Mustard Sauce

½ cup dry mustard
½ cup white vinegar
1 egg

½ cup sugar
cream cheese and crackers

Mix together dry mustard and wine vinegar. Let stand overnight or longer. Beat in egg and sugar. Cook in the top of a double boiler over boiling water for 18 minutes over high heat, stirring to prevent coagulation. Serve over cream cheese with crackers. This quantity of sauce will cover 4 to 8 ounces cream cheese and will keep for a couple of months in the refrigerator.

T H E   H O M E S T E A D   I N N

Les Huîtres des Gourmets

duxelles (see following
   recipe)

12 oysters on the half shell
3 tablespoons garlic butter

Place oysters on an oven-proof dish. Dab duxelles and garlic butter on each, and bake for 5 minutes. Serve garnished with lemon. Serves 4.

DUXELLES:

1 tablespoon butter
1 tablespoon minced onion
½ pound mushrooms,
   minced

1 tablespoon minced
   shallots
1 tablespoon heavy cream
salt and pepper to taste

Melt butter in sauté pan. Sauté onions until they begin to color. Add mushrooms and shallots and cook until liquids are rendered and then evaporate. Add a little cream and cook until reduced to a paste-like consistency. Season with salt and pepper to taste.

THE HOMESTEAD INN

Casserole d'Escargots

24 snails
5 ounces chanterelle
   mushrooms
1 tablespoon butter
2 teaspoons minced shallots

4 tablespoons garlic butter
½ cup heavy cream
½ teaspoon (a splash)
   Pernod (optional)

In a sauté pan, sauté snails and chanterelles in butter with shallots. Add garlic butter (see following recipe), let melt, and swirl around pan. Stir in heavy cream and Pernod and allow mixture to reduce somewhat. Sprinkle with chopped parsley and serve at once. Serves 4.

GARLIC BUTTER:

Mince large clove of garlic. Melt ¼ cup of softened butter in small pan. Add garlic, minced parsley, salt and pepper to taste.

HOMESTEAD INN
420 Field Point Road
Greenwich, Connecticut
06830
(203) 869-7500

All major credit cards
Very expensive

Built in 1799, the Homestead Inn is famous for its French cuisine and offers a weekend getaway from New York City, 45 miles away.

Homestead Inn
Greenwich, Connecticut

THE BRAMBLE INN

Caponata

2 pounds eggplant, peeled
    and cubed (½" cubes)
salt
½ cup olive oil
2 cups finely-chopped celery
¾ cup finely-chopped
    onions
⅓ cup wine vinegar mixed
    with 4 teaspoons sugar

3 cups drained whole-pack
    tomatoes
2 tablespoons tomato paste
6 large green olives, pitted
    and slivered
2 tablespoons capers
4 anchovy fillets, rinsed,
    pounded flat and smooth
freshly ground pepper

Sprinkle eggplant cubes generously with salt and set them in a colander to drain. After 35 minutes, pat cubes dry with paper towels and set aside. Heat ¼ cup olive oil in a heavy skillet. Add celery and cook for 10 minutes over moderate heat, stirring often. Stir in onions and cook for an additional 8 to 10 minutes, or until onions and celery are soft and lightly colored. With a slotted spoon transfer them to a bowl. Add remaining ¼ cup oil to skillet and sauté eggplant until it is lightly browned, stirring constantly. Return celery and onions to skillet. Add remaining ingredients. Bring to a boil and simmer uncovered for 15 minutes, stirring often. Flavor to taste with additional salt, pepper and vinegar. Refrigerate until ready to serve. Makes 8 cups, enough for 20 servings.

THE   BRAMBLE   INN

Best Liver Paté

¾ cup chopped scallions
1 clove garlic, minced
½ pound (2 sticks) butter
1 pound chicken livers
3 tablespoons cognac

⅛ teaspoon thyme
1½ teaspoons dry mustard
a dash each of nutmeg,
    cloves, mace
salt and pepper to taste

Sauté scallions and garlic in 3 tablespoons butter. Remove from pan. In same pan, sauté livers a few at a time in 2 table-spoons butter. Remove from sauté pan while slightly pink inside. Add cognac to pan. Ignite and pour over livers in an oven-proof dish. Put livers through fine-blade food grinder. Blend in the rest of the butter and spices. Add scallions and garlic and mix well. Season with salt and pepper to taste. Pour into mold. Chill until firm. To serve, unmold on platter or serve individual slices on bed of lettuce. Serves 12 to 15.

THE   INN   AT   PERRY   CABIN

Oysters Perry Cabin

40 fresh-shucked oysters on
    the half-shell
10 slices bacon, quartered

1½ cups grated cheddar
    cheese

Leave oysters on the deep side of the shell, discarding other half of shell. Top each oyster with a bit of cheese and a piece of bacon. Broil for 5 minutes, or until bacon is crisp. Serve immediately (you can serve on a bed of rock salt to help retain heat). Serves 6 to 8.

THE BRAMBLE INN
P.O. Box 807
Brewster, Massachusetts
02631
(508) 896–7644

MC / V / AE for meals only
Moderate

This Cape Cod inn is a haven for sports lovers, with the beach a 5-minute walk away, tennis courts adjacent, and golf and fishing nearby.

THE INN AT
PERRY CABIN
308 Watkins Lane
St. Michaels, Maryland
21663
(301) 745–5178

MC / V / AE
Very expensive

Situated on the serene Miles River in the historic village of St. Michaels, this 6-room inn offers guests nearby sailing, antiquing and spectacular water fowl watching.

OLD RITTENHOUSE
INN
301 Rittenhouse Avenue
Bayfield, Wisconsin
54814
(715) 779-5111

Moderate

This is an historic 30-room
mansion filled with an-
tiques and 12 working fireplaces. Put your feet up and
relax on the porch overlooking Lake Superior.

OLD RITTENHOUSE INN

Picante Cheesecake

1 pound Roquefort cheese
4 cups sour cream
2 cups grated Parmesan
 cheese

3 pounds cream cheese
2 cups picante sauce
16 eggs

Preheat oven to 350°. Prepare springform cheesecake pans by brushing with melted butter and lining with bread crumbs. This makes 4 cheesecakes, 11″ across.

Mix all ingredients. Pour into pans. Top with more bread crumbs. Bake at 350° for one hour and 15 minutes. Bake cheesecakes sitting in or on trays of water. Cool in oven for one hour with oven door ajar.

VICTORIAN FARMHOUSE

Toasted Clam Rolls

three 6½-ounce cans minced
 clams
⅓ cup thinly-sliced green
 onion
½ cup mayonnaise
6 tablespoons grated
 Parmesan cheese

1 teaspoon Worcestershire
 Sauce
¾ teaspoon garlic powder
½ teaspoon liquid hot pepper
 seasoning
1 large 24-ounce loaf thin-
 sliced sandwich bread
6 tablespoons melted butter

Preheat oven to 425°. Butter a baking sheet.

Drain clams well, reserving liquid for other cooking uses. Combine clams, green onions, mayonnaise, Parmesan cheese, Worcestershire Sauce, garlic powder and hot pepper seasoning.

VICTORIAN FARMHOUSE

Trim crusts from bread slices. With a rolling pin, flatten each slice until very thin. Spread about one tablespoon of clam mixture on each piece of bread, then roll up jellyroll fashion. Brush well with melted butter. Leave whole (for sandwiches) or cut in half (for appetizers). Arrange rolls 1" apart on baking sheet. Bake for 12 minutes, or until lightly browned. Makes 2 dozen finger sandwiches or 4 dozen appetizers.

BARNARD-GOOD HOUSE

Tom's Treat

4 juice oranges, squeezed
four 5½-ounce cans apricot
    nectar
2 fresh limes, squeezed
½ cup juice drained from
    crushed pineapple

6 tablespoons canned cream
    of coconut
1 cup vodka or rum
    (optional)

Mix all juices and shake well. Great for breakfast. For an evening drink, add crushed ice and vodka or rum. Serves 8.

The Barnard-Good House
Cape May, New Jersey

VICTORIAN FARMOUSE
P.O. Box 357
Little River, California
95456
(707) 937-0697

No credit cards
Expensive

This countryside inn is set among orchards and flower gardens.

BARNARD-GOOD
HOUSE
238 Perry Street
Cape May, New Jersey
08204
(609) 884-5381

MC/V
Expensive

Good breakfasts and warmth are the hallmarks of this resort-town inn, which also promises luxurious bathing in a copper tub.

FOOTHILL HOUSE

Smoked Salmon Appetizer

8 ounces cream cheese,
   softened
½ of a small onion, chopped
½ of a cube of butter, softened
8 ounces thinly sliced smoked
   salmon

½ of a small onion, thinly
   sliced
3 tablespoons capers
fresh dill to taste
mini bagels

Line a two cup fish mold with saran warp. Combine the cream cheese, chopped onion, and butter in a food processor. Line the fish mold with thinly sliced salmon encasing the mold, a layer of the cream cheese mixture, a layer of sliced onion, and a tablespoon of the capers. Repeat with remaining cream cheese, layer of smoked salmon, layer of onion and capers, ending with the smoked salmon. Completely cover the mold with saran wrap.

Refrigerate the fish mold up to a day ahead. Invert the mold on a serving dish. Remove the saran wrap and garnish the mold with the remaining thinly sliced onion, capers, and dill. Serve with mini bagels.

FOOTHILL HOUSE
3037 Foothill Boulevard
Calistoga, California
94515
(800) 942-6933
(707) 942-6933

MC/V/AE
Expensive

Located in a country setting, Foothill House offers three spacious rooms individually decorated with antiques, each with a private bath, entrance and fireplace. A separate elegant cottage is available.

Foothill House
Calistoga, California

THE VERMONT INN
Bloody Mary

2 cups V-8 Juice
2 ounces lemon and lime
    juice, mixed
2 teaspoons horseradish
4 dashes of Tabasco Sauce
4 dashes of Worcestershire
    Sauce

¼ teaspoon celery salt
¼ teaspoon salt
¼ teaspoon pepper
6 ounces vodka
4 wedges lime
4 stalks celery

Mix V-8 Juice with lemon-lime mix, horseradish, Tabasco and Worcestershire sauces, salt, pepper and vodka. Shake with cracked ice and strain to 4 large glasses over ice cubes. Garnish each with a wedge of lime and stalk of celery.

Serves 4.

Mussels Dijon

2 dozen mussels
1 tablespoon olive oil
1 tablespoon garlic, minced
¼ cup sliced Spanish onions
dash of white wine

1 tablespoon Dijon style
    mustard
½ cup heavy cream
½ cup clam juice

De-beard and rinse mussels. Heat a large sauté pan to 425 degrees. Place oil in pan and sauté garlic and onions. Deglaze pan with splash of white wine and add in mustard. Place mussels in pan, along with cream and clam juice. Top with a second pan to create steam.

Reduce heat slightly and steam for 5 minutes. Mussels are done when they open. Serve with crackers or favorite bread.

Serves 2.

THE VERMONT INN
Route 4, Box 37J
Killington, Vermont
05751
(802) 775-0708

MC/V/AE
Expensive

The Vermont Inn is a favorite for winter vacations, with the Killington and Pico ski areas just minutes away. Rates are lower in summer, when the tennis courts and swimming pool are enticing attractions.

Index